Rob Mallernee

THE PROS PRAISE

QUANTUM GOLF

"BOTH PRACTICAL AND ENTERTAINING... it demonstrates that the secret to good golf is sometimes backing off from your game and having fun with it."

—Bill Davis, Master Professional, Jupiter Hills Golf Club

➤

"ENLIGHTENING... able to penetrate the real heart of the matter... I felt as if the author had actually accompanied me on my quest for excellence.... The lessons Enhager offers are those which have enabled me to excel at the game."

—Jane Blalock, LPGA champion

➤

"The very rich and natural experience of quantum golf brings relief and success to the frustrated golfer. It offers a more accomplished player the final stroke of fulfillment."

—Mary Ann Williams, LPGA Teaching Division Instructor

➤

"INTERESTING... ENJOYABLE.... The teaching concepts are completely valid."
—Jim Flick, Teaching Professional, The Golf Club at Desert Mt.

➤

"HIGHLY ENTERTAINING... profoundly simple and simply profound—advice that will improve your golf game but can also be applied to life."
—Willis Harman, author of *Global Mind Change*

➤

"DELIGHTFUL... FUN AND VERY USEFUL. You will learn to turn the frustrations of golf—and life—into a joyous, effortless discipline."
—Harold H. Bloomfield, M.D., author of *Inner Joy* and *The Achilles Syndrome*

➤

"The message of QUANTUM GOLF is the ideal medicine.... It goes beyond the mechanics of the game to the power of human consciousness."
—Larry Dossey, M.D., author of *Recovering the Soul* and *Space, Time, Medicine*

➤

THE PATH TO GOLF MASTERY

QUANTUM GOLF

KJELL ENHAGER

A Time Warner Company

Warner Books, Inc., 1271 Avenue of the Americas, New York, NY 10020

Printed in the United States of America
First trade printing: June 1992
10 9 8 7 6

Library of Congress Cataloging-in-Publication Data

Enhager, Kjell.
Quantum golf : the path to golf mastery / by Kjell Enhager.
p. cm.
Includes bibliographical references (p.).
ISBN 0-446-39196-4
1. Golf—Psychological aspects. 2. Visualization. I. Title.
GV979.P75E54 1991
796.352'01—dc20 90-50526
CIP

Book design by Giorgetta Bell McRee
Illustrations by Judy Pedersen
Cover design by Jackie Merri Meyer
Cover illustration by Christopher Zacharow

Wherein an ordinary player learns that the course is the world,
that the game is a process,
and that, in order to "win,"
the person with the club must be no more and no less
than a part of nature . . .

CONTENTS

ACKNOWLEDGMENTS

If this book gives you pleasure as well as information then Samantha Wallace's skills as both a storyteller and a writer are evident. Her warmth and humor are on every page.

I would also like to thank my editor, Rick Horgan, for his perceptive suggestions; and my agent, Muriel Nellis, for her support and guidance.

PROLOGUE

Glinting in the sun, the polished steel shaft of the club turned lazily end on end against the sky. At its highest point it appeared to be in slow motion, but it was actually traveling at an enormous velocity.

"That's it!" John Smith screamed hoarsely. "I quit!"

He punctuated his words by hurling his sand wedge, then scooped up his handmade leather golf bag and held it above his head, looking like a slightly flabby Conan the Barbarian.

"C'mon, J.S.," said his head accountant and golf partner. "You don't really mean that."

"Oh, *yeah*?" Smith stalked down the slope of the green to a deep water hazard. "I can't play golf without clubs," he bellowed. With a satisfied grunt, Smith heaved his remaining thirteen clubs and their container into the pond. A spume of water rose into the air as if a depth charge had exploded.

"That's it," he growled and started for the clubhouse. "If you want a guy who can engineer a corporate takeover, I'm your man. If you want a guy who can beat the stock market, I'm your man. But if you want someone who can hit a little white ball, *don't call me!*"

Smith was trembling as he staggered into the club. He'd been to the greatest golf schools in America and spent thousands of dollars on hand-crafted, counterweighted clubs constructed of Space Age materials, but in the end it all came down to hitting a little white ball.

Supporting himself against the wall, he made it to his locker and slumped down on the bench, burying his face in his hands. Moisture that could as easily have been tears of frustration as perspiration trickled between his fingers. He felt someone sit beside him.

"John?"

It was Herbert Wooly, the club pro. Wiry and wise, he was an ancient veteran of the links. Smith's face remained buried in his hands. "I can't make it, Herb," he said. "I'm giving up."

"I know how you feel," Herb soothed. "But there's one thing I have to tell you. You have a great enthusiasm for the game—maybe too much enthusiasm. Anyway, I think you've reached that emotional place where you're ready to accept a tip I've only given twice before. I wouldn't suggest it except that you're so desperate. Now . . . maybe . . . you'll listen."

In spite of himself, Smith was curious. "What is it?"

"Go to Iowa."

Smith's head jerked up. He turned on the wizened pro. "Iowa!" His eyes were wild. He banged his fist into the locker. "My life is coming apart. For the first time since I could tie my own shoes I've failed completely, and you're talking to me about Iowa?"

"There's a great teacher out there."

"Where?" Smith's voice was acid. "In the cornfields? I've *had* the best teachers money can buy."

"I know, I know. You've had the best conventional teachers, but this man is a world apart."

"He's in another world, all right," said Smith. "Iowa."

Herb pressed on. "It's worth the trip, I guarantee. As I told you, there are only two other people I've mentioned this to, and one of them flew to Iowa to see this teacher and went from a fifteen handicap to scratch."

"Yeah? What about the other guy?"

"He never went," Herb said sadly, "but he should have."

Herb paused a moment, then said, "Look, John, this teacher has a completely new approach to the game. It's more profound than anything I've ever heard of, and I'm convinced he can help anyone at any level. I *know* he can help you. He teaches something called Quantum Golf."

"Quantum Golf?"

The old man nodded. "Quantum Golf."

"What's that supposed to mean?"

"Don't ask me," Herb said. "Ask him."

"Well, what's his name?"

"Linc St. Clair."

"How come I've never heard of him?"

The pro shrugged. "He's kind of a recluse. Lives on a farm outside a little town called Fairfield. He runs the farm himself and teaches a few of the top touring pros on the side."

Narrowing his eyes, Smith regarded the old professional. "If he's so good, why is he still out in the sticks?"

"He won't leave," Herb smiled. "He calls it heaven on earth."

Smith snorted. There was a long silence between them.

"Will you see him?" Herb asked.

"In Iowa? You've got to be kidding!"

QUANTUM GOLF

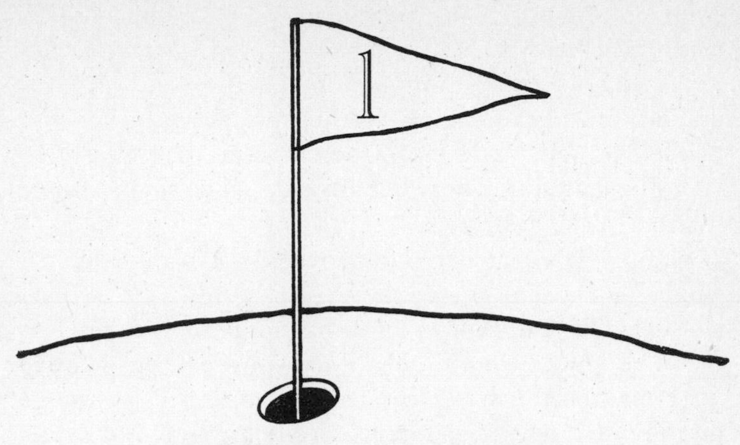

FRAME OF MIND: THE QUANTUM WORLD

The shiny corporate Lear jet squealed as it landed and skidded toward a cornfield at the extreme end of the short runway. At the last second just before ten rows of corn were harvested early, the pilot was able to slow the plane sufficiently to turn to the side and then back to what passed for a hangar in the little airport.

John Smith called heartily to his two-person crew, "Told you we'd make it."

Waiting beside the hangar was an old yellow Chevy in excellent condition, the words FAIRFIELD TAXI stenciled in red across its front doors.

As Smith climbed down from the plane he muttered under his breath. "Only transportation in town is this one-horse taxi service. Whoever heard of this place, anyway?"

He got into the cab. The driver was a red-haired

woman. She turned her fiery head and gave him a homey smile. "Where to?"

"The golf club," Smith commanded.

She revved the engine. "Which one?"

He sneered. "You mean there's more than one?"

"There are three here in Fairfield," she said in a bored voice. "Take your pick."

Smith glared at her. He growled, "I want Linc St. Clair."

"Oh. Do you want to go to his home or the club?"

"The club," Smith said, "but"—he paused—"drive past his home first." He'd found it a useful technique in judging a person to appraise his home before meeting him. He leaned back against the vinyl car seat as they passed fields of corn alternating with soybeans and farmhouses whose weathered barns were surrounded by mudyards that were universally populated with pigs—or were they hogs? Smith wondered what the difference was. Whatever they were, the creatures were omnipresent and Iowa was a far cry from Manhattan.

The taxi pulled onto the side of the road. Tall trees led up a hill where centennial oaks allowed only glimpses of a large brick house. Smith could just make out its general shape and some of its Victorian wooden trim.

"There it is," nodded the driver.

"Uh, can't we get a closer look?"

She eyed Smith in her rearview mirror. "Yeah, I suppose so." She swung the steering wheel to the right. Slowly they climbed the shaded path; as the house came into full view, they eased to a stop.

"That's as close as I'm goin'. Mr. Linc lives out here for his privacy."

There were two large dogs on the porch. The more grizzled of the two rose lazily and ambled down wide stone steps to check out the newcomers. As it neared the car, it barked dutifully.

In a frantic fanning of feathers, a peacock flew from an overhanging branch and landed lightly on the hood of the taxi. It spread its tail in glorious display. Smith stared. A strange gobbling noise broke his concentration. Three fantailed turkeys waddled noisily down the lane, the younger dog trotting behind them. He stopped beside his pal. The dogs peered interestedly into the car.

Smith looked down at them. After a moment he said, "We might as well go to the club." Was this St. Clair guy a farmer or a zookeeper? Smith's hopes for his lessons were not high.

"Okay, mister. It's your trip," the redhead said as she looked over her shoulder and backed down the lane to the highway.

Smith sat in silence. What kind of a golf professional was this Linc St. Clair?

The approach to the Royal Master's Golf Club was bordered in lush flowering bushes. The fieldstone clubhouse, with its expensive glazed green tile roof was reminiscent of an English country manor. The country house theme was repeated indoors with rich mahogany furnishings and elegant oriental carpeting.

Smith whistled tunelessly. *I don't think we're in Kansas anymore, Toto.*

Behind a marble-topped front desk sat a young man with very wavy hair. "How can I help you, sir?"

Smith regained command. "I just flew in from New York to take a lesson from your Mr. St. Clair," he said.

"Oh, I'm very sorry, sir, you should have called." The man shrugged apologetically. "You see, he's booked for the next four and a half years."

"What?" Smith's eyes popped. "Four and a half

years!" His jaw thrust forward aggressively. "Look here, young man. I want to speak to the manager. You tell him John Paul Smith is here."

"*The* Mr. John Paul Smith?" Smith heard the familiar tone of recognition and awe in the young man's voice.

"In the flesh."

"All right! Yes, sir!" the young man replied, and rushed through an oak-paneled door directly behind the counter.

Smith's cheeks were flushed. I should have asked to speak to the manager first, he thought. You can only accomplish what you want by going to the top.

A large, pleasant-faced man appeared behind the front desk. "Can I help you, Mr. Smith?" His tone was benign. "My name is Jim Smilek. I'm the manager here."

"See here, Smilek, I came all the way from New York to get a lesson from your Mr. St. Clair. I'd like you to arrange it." Smith slowly withdrew five crisp one-hundred-dollar bills, one after the other from his billfold and set them on the edge of the desk.

The manager spread his hands in an expansive gesture of apology. "I'm *very* sorry, sir, but I can't accept your generous tip. Mr. St. Clair really *is* booked up."

Just then the young curly-haired man joined his boss behind the counter. "Mr. Smilek, wait," he said. "We've just had a cancellation. Mr. Finley broke his leg and can't come."

"Well," replied Mr. Smilek, "that's extraordinary, Mr. Smith. We don't keep a set waiting list here. If there's a cancellation it's first come, first served."

Mr. Smith seized the moment. "Good," he said. "It's about time." With one hand he scooped the bills off the counter and stuffed them into his pocket. "When can we get this lesson going? I have to be back in New York tonight."

"Oh," said the manager. "Perhaps you weren't informed. Mr. St. Clair only takes students for a minimum one-week series of lessons. That way he can give his full attention to his students as well as to the management of his farm."

"The guy's a farmer, eh? Is he any good?" Smith queried.

"Yes," the manager replied. "He is one of the most successful farmers in the county. He also has Sika deer, peacocks, llamas, endurance Arabians, and Peruvian Paso Finos, and he raises the finest Morgan horses in the Midwest."

Smith's mouth, which had dropped during the manager's recitation, closed. He was for once speechless. He shook his head abruptly like a dog bothered by flies.

"Now, Mr. Smith, to get back to your lesson," the manager added smoothly. "Please let us know if the week-long lesson will be convenient for you. Mr. Jones asked me to call him immediately if there was a cancellation."

"Jones, eh?" Smith's competitive juices immediately began flowing. "Well, I'm certainly not going to let him have this spot. I'll take it."

"Very good," the manager said and extended a dark green, gold-embossed register for him to sign. Besides space for the usual information, Smith noticed a line on which he was to record his golf handicap. For a brief moment he considered lying, then he scrawled the correct figure on the appropriate line and tossed the pen aside.

"So," he said, rubbing his hands together, "when do I meet this Mr. St. Clair? I want to get started."

"He's at the range now. Why don't we go on out?" Smilek indicated a driving range that lay outside beyond a set of tall French doors.

Smith began to follow but then stopped abruptly. "Oh, I'll need to buy a new set of clubs."

"No problem," Smilek said amiably. "Let's go into the pro shop." They walked a few feet off the lobby into a plush, well-stocked golf shop.

"We have a variety here—Taylor, Ping, MacGregor, Wilson, Slotline, some of the new Japanese clubs . . . You can choose any of them. It's all included."

For the first time since he had entered the building, Mr. Smith smiled. He pointed to a set of expensive clubs and a handmade bag of soft, dark leather. "I'll try these new graphites," he said cheerfully, slapping the manager on his broad back. "Let's go."

They walked out the back door of the clubhouse, the manager shouldering Smith's new clubs. They followed a winding path of crushed white shell through a bed of antique roses.

Not bad, Smith thought, for Iowa. Beyond the garden lay a large, beautifully tended practice green for putting. He noticed that each hole had its own miniature pin consisting of a small green and white flag waving crisply from a polished brass pole. As they walked toward the driving range, they could hear a heavy, regular, thudding sound.

"What's that banging?" Smith asked.

"Oh," the manager replied nonchalantly, "that must be Mr. St. Clair hitting balls."

Smith looked at him sharply. That noise was *loud*. They passed through an imposing yew hedge that separated the putting green from the driving range and his eye was caught by the sheer energy of a ball in flight. It arced high toward an expanse of lush grass unfolding for several hundred yards like an emerald carpet broken only by staggered white distance markers. Beyond that lay a view of undulating hills shaded here and there with stands of giant oak rich in their summer foliage.

At the range, with his driver poised back over his left shoulder, his back arched, and his right foot lightly balanced on the toes was the compact, sturdy figure of Linc St. Clair.

The man seemed unusually well formed and balanced, Smith thought, as if nature had decided for once to allot a human being perfect proportions. He filed the impression.

The teacher turned to them. His skin was a rosy, healthy bronze, and his blue eyes radiated a vast reserve of energy that Smith had recognized before in people who were brilliantly successful: those who were not only intelligent but able to act coherently with their intelligence, bringing themselves almost unlimited success at whatever they touched. Smith wondered if a man who had chosen to be a farmer and live as a golf professional in what appeared to be a virtual backwater could be such a phenomenon.

Okay, he thought, he'd reserve judgment on that one. He was perplexed by the man's age though. This fellow could be anything from twenty-five to sixty-three. He was either prematurely gray or extremely well preserved.

As they came closer Smith could see St. Clair was using his driver and seemed to be aiming at a 300-yard sign. The ball flew like a missile and slammed into the metal sign, falling directly to the ground beneath and adding to a mound of some thirty other balls. Smith's mind fought with his eyes.

The manager introduced them. "Mr. St. Clair, this is your new student, Mr. John Smith."

Linc St. Clair gave a wide smile and promptly extended his hand. "How nice to meet you," he said.

Smilek continued, "Mr. Finley had an unfortunate accident and was unable to make it. Mr. Smith would like to fill in for him. He is an amateur from New York with a handicap of . . ." The manager's voice diplomatically dropped out of hearing.

Smith frowned. He said briskly, "Let's get started, shall we?"

"Why don't you show me your swing, Mr. Smith?" St. Clair suggested.

The manager handed Smith the brilliant new clubs and Smith selected a metal driver. After plucking a range ball from a nearby bucket, he went through his procedure of setting up to the ball. After a few waggles of the club, he whacked the ball soundly. The ball flew straight and then curved to the right, landing nearly 175 yards out into the verdant grass.

Smith's face strained. "It's my right side again," he said. "I just can't seem to release." A muscle in his jaw twitched. "I just can't hit very far. When I play with my friends they always outdrive me. Frankly, I find it humiliating"—he gave the pro a steely glance—"and I want something done about it."

"Maybe we should start from the beginning," Linc said as he pulled a seven iron from the bag and handed it to him. "Warm up with this, it's easier than a driver."

Except for the clear call of birds, there was quiet in the fields around them. Mr. Smith gripped the seven iron and began to hit ball after ball. The shots scattered out in front of the 150-yard marker. St. Clair motioned for him to stop. The teacher's eyes crinkled into a smile. "In its essence," he said, "golf is a simple game."

Smith's attempt to laugh burst from his mouth like the bark of a crazed Doberman.

"You're trying too hard," St. Clair said. "Everything

looks good as far as your technique and fundamentals go, but you're not allowing yourself to swing naturally."

Smith pulled a linen handkerchief from his hip pocket and wiped his face.

"Let's use the image of dancing," Linc said. "When you learned to dance you started first by learning the steps."

"Yeah?" Smith said, partially in agreement and partially in impatience.

"After a while," Linc continued, "you had familiarized yourself with the basic moves, and you didn't have to pay attention to them anymore; you just needed to listen to the rhythm of the music."

His pupil's jaw jutted forward. "That's true."

"If you had been continually concerned about the steps, you would never be able to dance very well."

Again Smith had to agree.

"And if you were paying attention to your feet, you'd be stiff and jerky, out of rhythm."

"I guess . . ." Smith's thoughts twined together, and on that thread he climbed mentally to relatively pleasant memories of the dance floor.

"When you dance well, you're in tune with the music. There's no thought about the steps, you're only aware of flowing with the rhythm."

Smith nodded.

"Okay," Linc said. "It's the same with a golf swing. After you've familiarized yourself with the basics of classical golf, you have to stop putting your attention on the steps. Your emphasis must be on the flow, on the rhythm of your swing."

Smith felt that St. Clair was minimizing his problem, and told him so. "You make it sound pretty easy."

"It is. Flow and feeling are the glue that sticks everything together. They make the whole of your swing bigger than the sum of its parts. When you swing correctly, it is totally effortless and natural. It shouldn't tire you out to play golf," he said. "Every time you swing, instead of *losing* energy, you should *gain* it. After all, the real reason we play golf is because of the happiness we get from it, isn't that right?"

Smith looked at him, not comprehending.

St. Clair's blue eyes were mischievous as he asked, "Would you mind taking out your favorite club?"

"Favorite club? All right, that would be my three wood. I always hit well with that. I dunno why, but I can hit off the fairway perfectly with this baby. Well"—Smith qualified his boldness—"almost perfectly. Now and then I make a mistake—but no big deal."

"I see," remarked St. Clair.

Smith reached for his three wood and quickly set up to the ball. He proceeded to hit a smooth 210-yard draw. Teacher and pupil stared after it.

Smith looked hopefully toward his mentor. After a moment of silence, St. Clair said, "That's very good. Do you swing like that often?"

"Mostly with my three wood, and once in a while with my irons." He snorted out a short laugh. "One day I think I've finally solved the great mystery of golf, and the next day I'm in deep woods—and I do mean woods! I just can't seem to be consistent."

"A lot of people have one or two clubs they really like and do well with, but they can't play consistently with all their clubs. It's actually a common problem in the world today."

Smith heard him say, "You've put your trust in classical golf."

"*Classical* golf, you say?" Smith's eyebrows rose. He stared at the golf teacher, whose hair shone in the sunlight, creating somewhat of a halo effect.

"Yes," the pro repeated.

Smith's voice was hoarse with repressed impatience, "What *should* I be doing?"

Linc looked at him squarely. "You should be playing Quantum Golf."

"What in blue blazes is Quantum Golf?"

"Actually," his teacher said, "you know all there is to know about Quantum Golf already."

"I do?"

"Yes, you do," he said. "It's just that you don't trust in it. Your belief system is still classical, especially when you're using your driver."

Smith's eyebrows shot up again. "It is?"

"When you use your three wood," Linc explained, "then you've started playing Quantum Golf."

"I don't get it. It's my grip, isn't it? With the three wood I have a better grip, right?"

"No." St. Clair shook his head. "Grip is a consideration of classical golf. You have an excellent grip. I do recommend that everyone learn the traditional, classical fundamentals of golf, but to tell you the truth, I've had students who have unconventional grips who can still hit the ball very well. Each of us has our own internal rhythm, our own unique style. This doesn't mean that we shouldn't learn certain classical fundamentals of golf. For a single shot it doesn't matter what grip you have, but in order to play well consistently it's obviously better to have the right grip."

Smith nodded eagerly. "Then it's my setup. One instructor told me that my feet were too far apart. That's probably the reason I hit the driver so poorly."

"No," the teacher said. "Your setup and alignment look excellent. Most of your basics are fine. Your feet are about the width of your shoulders, and the ball is aligned toward the inside of your left foot. You've had some good teachers." He grinned. "Good classical golf teachers, that is."

Frowning, Smith bit the edge of his lip hard. "It must be something to do with my swing mechanics."

"No." St. Clair was firm. Twin blue lasers focused on Smith, who felt almost paralyzed by the intensity of the gaze.

"Perhaps I'm not making myself clear," the teacher said. "You keep referring to classical golf. In my school, classical golf fundamentals are an important part of the game, but only a part. You have to have a complete approach. You must go beyond the classical fundamentals. They are like learning the steps in dancing—you have to go beyond the basic steps and listen to the music. If you want to learn more classical golf"—he shrugged—"then I suggest another school. I teach Quantum Golf."

"Quantum . . . ," Smith repeated numbly. "I'll stick with you for now," he said, hating himself for this brief, uncharacteristic moment of humility.

Linc smiled serenely. "Then I'll be happy to give you your first lesson."

"I'm ready," Smith said, his jaw firmly clamped against his upper teeth.

"Okay. The first lesson is called **frame of mind.**"

His jaw fell. "What?" He shut it quickly.

"Frame of mind. You can choose either a classical frame of mind or a quantum frame of mind. It's kind of a belief system, not unlike a world view. Every human being chooses one or the other. If a golfer takes the classical frame of mind, then he cannot play from the quantum mechanical level. However, when you picked up your three wood you unconsciously put away classical thinking and classical fears." Linc gestured. "At that moment you were able to trust in the quantum world. Do you see?"

Smith frowned. "I never even passed physics. I haven't the foggiest idea what you mean by 'classical' and 'quantum.' "

Linc laughed. "It's just nature. Physics is simply how nature works. When you're a farmer, you live with nature every day. A farmer's livelihood is mixed up with the soil, the sun, the rain, with the seasons. It's just natural to want to understand it. But you don't have to know about physics to play Quantum Golf. Let me explain a few basic principles that might make it easier to understand the difference between the classical and quantum worlds."

Linc warmed to his explanation. "When a physicist talks about the classical world he's referring to the familiar world around us, the world we've always known—a concrete, solid world that we were taught to think of as being constructed from atoms, or tiny particles of matter."

He looked at his student to determine how much he was taking in. Smith nodded in silent response. He did not sit on the board of several Fortune 500 companies by being unintelligent.

St. Clair continued, "The quantum world is the same world, but seen in its completeness. It not only includes the visible, manifest layers of nature, but its hidden, unmanifest layers as well. The word *quantum* means the smallest unit of nature, the tiniest level of transition. At this fine level everything looks and behaves very differently from the classical level. Nothing is solid and static. It's a world of infinite energy and dynamism. One minute a particle is a particle, the next minute it is a wave, and then it's just a bump in a vast unbounded field. In the quantum world the field, the wholeness, is everything —an unmanifest, unified field that lies at the basis of nature."

"Just where did you learn all this?" Smith asked.

"Oh, there's a university right down the road there, in town. A young professor from Harvard runs the physics department. I've taken a few classes there." St. Clair chuckled. "Mostly I just sit around with the professors and discuss the relative and the absolute. I find most of their ideas are really common sense. Which, of course," he said gently, "isn't all that common."

"Yeah, well"—Smith's brows pressed heavily upon his eyes—"I'd like to know how all this is going to help my game."

"Let me explain it simply in terms of golf."

"Please do."

"First," Linc said, "classical golf emphasizes the parts of the swing rather than the whole." The Iowan was clearly enthusiastic, but Smith resisted his energy.

The teacher continued. "You learn about each aspect of the swing and then separately try to improve them. If something goes wrong when you're playing golf, the common approach is to try and find out which part of the swing is wrong and then correct it. Your attention is always on analyzing the part— Is my grip right? Is my right side too strong—" He didn't get a chance to finish his sentence.

"What's wrong with that?" Smith thundered. "Are you saying classical fundamentals aren't important?"

"No," Linc assured, "they have their place, and there they are important, but they give an incomplete picture. In the classical frame of mind attention goes to the outer, physical level. The ball is hard, the club is steel, and so we feel we have to hold the club tightly and swing hard. In Quantum Golf our attention is not actually on the ball."

Oh great! Smith thought.

"It's not on any part of the swing," his teacher continued, "or on any particular part of our body. We don't worry, 'Is my left arm straight? Is my weight shifting?' When you're in a quantum frame of mind," he explained, "your attention shifts to a more complete picture—to the whole of the swing. The parts are included, but they are a secondary consideration. It is the *whole* swing and the inner rhythm of that whole swing that is all-important. We no longer think of the body or the muscles—we put our attention on the inner flow of consciousness."

"Flow of consciousness? I have to tell you, St. Clair, I wouldn't know the flow of consciousness from a floral arrangement. I can't really see how this frame of mind thing can make that big a difference. I mean it's just an attitude, right?"

Linc looked at him for a long moment. In spite of himself Smith began to feel uncomfortable.

"Here, take this club," Linc said, handing him his three wood. Smith casually extended his hand and held the club in an easy manner. His body was relaxed, his stance was perfect.

"Do you want me to swing now?" he asked.

"That won't be necessary." Linc smiled and took the three wood from him. He passed Smith a driver. "Let's try this one."

Immediately Smith's body changed. As he addressed the ball, his body stiffened and his shoulders contracted and rose toward his neck, giving him a hunched appearance. He gripped the club tightly. "Shall I hit now?"

"Do you notice any difference between this club and the other one I handed you?" Linc asked.

"No. . . . Well," he amended, "maybe this one is a little heavier."

"Try to pay attention this time to how your body feels when I hand you each club."

"My body?"

"Yes." The teacher exchanged Smith's driver for his three wood. Without noticing it Smith released a sigh and his shoulders resumed their natural position. He stood easily, his feet apart, well balanced, holding the club in a relaxed, yet controlled manner.

"How does your body feel now?"

"Fine."

"Good," Linc said. He took the three wood from him again and exchanged it for the driver. Smith's body contorted in tension. Again his shoulders rose in tension, and he held the driver in a death grip.

"Do you notice any difference between how you feel now and how you felt holding your three wood?"

Smith stared down at his hands, which were clenched around the club.

"I seem to be holding the club too tightly." They could both plainly see the whitened knuckles of Smith's hand.

"That's true," Linc agreed. "Anything else?"

"My stomach feels kind of tight, too."

Linc smiled gently. "It would help if you breathed."

Smith let out a mighty breath, "Ah . . ." His shoulders relaxed as he exhaled. He laughed. "That's amazing. It's like I'm two different people, depending upon which club I'm holding."

"Yes," Linc said. "When I handed you the driver you believed that this club had to hit the ball a maximum distance plus an extra twenty yards for good measure. This means that you really believed you had to put effort into your swing. You started to grip hard, you tensed your arms, tightened your shoulders, stiffened your neck, and"—he paused significantly—"you stopped breathing. In other words, you stopped the flow. The mechanics of your swing depended completely on your belief system!"

"Now that you point it out," Smith said, "I can see it."

"The moment you picked up your three wood you relaxed, you breathed again and forgot all about swing mechanics. For that single moment your intellect stopped obstructing your body. You simply held the thought, 'I can hit the ball perfectly with this club.' You know a three wood won't hit the ball as far as a driver, so you tend to swing easier with it. Whatever the reason, you have developed confidence with this club, and when you swing with it your mind allows your body to have an effortless, smooth swing."

"All that was going on?"

"Yes. In Quantum Golf the focus is on allowing this automatic procedure to happen *every time*. Somewhere inside us, each of us already has the perfect swing. Every golfer has his own perfect golf swing, according to that person's individual constitution, physiology, psychology, and temperament. The thing each of us has to do is find it."

"How?" Smith demanded, his arms folded firmly in front of him in a classically defensive pose.

"How do we find it? Well, you've already shown me that you have it. Now it's my task to educate you so that you can maintain this same mind-set, this same knowledge or belief with every club you pick up, every shot you take, not only with your three wood but also with your driver," Linc said. "You will simply bccomc familiar, intimate even"—he grinned—"with the five fundamentals of Quantum Golf."

"The five fundamentals?"

"Yes, and you've already learned the first one."

"I have?"

"You have," Linc confirmed. "Remember **frame of mind**?"

"Yeah, but what am I supposed to do?"

"Lock up your driver."

Smith was aghast. "Lock up my big dog?"

"Lock it up," St. Clair said firmly. "Put it away so you can't even see it. Forget it."

"Forever?"

"For a little while," Linc relented. "But we can't continue with the lessons until you lock up your driver. As long as it's anywhere around, you will be bound by classical thinking about distance and power. We want to create the right environment for your growth and allow you to become firmly established in your new style of playing. The temptation to hit the ball for distance and power is just too great." He smiled and looked at the New York executive for a long time without a word. It occurred to Smith that he would not like to face Linc across a negotiating table.

St. Clair finally broke the silence. "Mr. Smith"—he was every ounce the professional now—"I don't want to see you play with a driver until I say so. When the time is right I want to share that moment with you. I don't want you to even have a driver in your bag. Is that clear?"

Smith nodded but he was worried.

"Right," Linc said. "That's it for today."

Smith was incredulous. "That's it? That's the whole first lesson?"

"Yes," the pro smiled. "As the week goes on we'll

consider the other four fundamentals of Quantum Golf."

"And what are they?"

"Don't worry about them now." St. Clair's tone was reassuring. "We'll consider each of them in a very simple and complete manner."

Smith was still a little concerned. "It all seems kind of abstract to me."

"I assure you, Mr. Smith, it's very concrete." The teacher grinned at him. "Have fun playing golf tomorrow morning. But remember today's lesson."

Smith cocked his head. "Which was?"

"Frame of mind. Learn to recognize whether you're swinging the club quantum mechanically or classically. If you're swinging quantum mechanically, you'll actually gain energy from your golf swing and feel energetic afterward. If you're swinging classically, you'll be a little more tired and strained afterward. The feeling you have when you hit your three wood is the feeling of the Quantum swing. When you pick up this club, you're not thinking about details of the swing, only how easy and smooth it is. You have the wholeness of the swing in your mind."

Smith nodded, clinging to the memory of that feeling.

Linc continued, "All of us have a few classical golf habits that are hard to break. Change depends on several factors. For instance, the benefits that you recognize you can achieve through change, as well as how committed you are to making the change. The transition from the classic to the quantum isn't immediate, but it should be fun. With each lesson you'll see how effortless your Quantum swing will become. Okay, Mr. Smith. That's it for the day."

St. Clair shaded his eyes with his hand and studied the sun. "It's three fifty-one now," he said, "and I have an appointment with seven hundred cows who are waiting to move to their summer pasture."

Smith noticed that the teacher wore no watch. He looked down at his own wristwatch: It was exactly three fifty-one. How had St. Clair done that? he wondered.

Linc added an afterthought. "Don't worry," he said, "if you find yourself going through some classical golf–withdrawal symptoms; it's just part of the process. I'll see you tomorrow afternoon. Now enjoy."

An appointment with cows? Smith shuddered. And "classical golf–withdrawal symptoms"? What in blue blazes was he in for?

Practice Drills for Chapter 1

1. Watch people take their swing and recognize the difference between classical and quantum. See if the swing is effortless or strained; see if there is a smooth rhythm to their swing.

2. Notice if your own swing is classical or quantum. Is your swing totally effortless? Do you gain energy from each swing?

3. If you're a complete beginner and are unfamiliar with such fundamentals of golf as grip, setup, etc., you should take a series of basic lessons from a qualified PGA or LPGA instructor. It will also be helpful to read Ben Hogan's *Five Lessons: The Modern Fundamentals of Golf* several times over. This is the best introduction to the classical fundamentals.

FLOW: THE SUPERFLUID QUANTUM SWING

On a carved teak bench beside the practice range, Linc sat upright with his eyes closed, his legs crossed under him.

Smith blinked as he approached. Was that daylight he saw between St. Clair and the bench?

It seemed to be daylight! What the Sam Hill was going on here? Was the man floating?

He leaned over and squinted. No, Linc was doing nothing but sitting quietly. Smith blotted his brow with his wilted handkerchief—this place must be affecting him.

The teacher opened his blue eyes and casually reached for a large and venerable Stetson straw hat perched on the bench beside him. He placed it on his head; Smith eyed the brilliant peacock feather waving from its hatband.

"How was your game today, Mr. Smith?" the pro asked.

Smith pulled his eyes from the feather, his shoulders slumped.

"Terrible." He sat down beside Linc. "I got a fifty-three on the front nine and a forty-six on the back. I've never played worse. Quantum Golf stinks."

"I see," Linc said, laughing. "Hand me that club, will you?"

"You mean this one?" Smith held up a thin-bladed putter.

"Yes, that will be fine." St. Clair walked the few feet to the practice area and teed up a ball. With the most truly effortless swing Smith had ever witnessed, the teacher hit the ball, as if he were sweeping a floor rather than swinging a golf club. The ball started low over the fine green turf and then rose in the air toward the large cumulus clouds that floated like great icebergs in the sky. It touched the ground past the 250-yard mark.

Smith gazed in amazement. "I'll bet you putt with your driver," he said.

"Why yes," the teacher replied, as if Smith had been serious. "That can be a challenge."

Smith couldn't help but wonder what universe this guy came from. He probed, "I don't think I've ever tried that one, Mr. St. Clair."

"I like to challenge myself," St. Clair said. "It helps break boundaries." He looked at Smith. "I'm sure you're a man who likes to break boundaries."

"I used to think so," Smith said. He was baffled by this man. He simply had never met anyone quite like him. And that darn peacock feather was distracting.

"Let's get back to your game, Mr. Smith. Did anything at all go well today? Did you gain energy from any of your golf swings?"

"Actually"—Smith reflected for a moment—"I did hit my three wood extremely well, although I couldn't hit anything else."

"I see," the teacher responded.

Smith snorted happily. "One of the other players even said that with my three wood I had the swing of Sam Snead."

"Has anyone ever commented on your swing before?"

"Well, I've played with some pros who say that when I'm really on with my three wood it's the best swing they've ever seen. Ah, I don't really believe them. After five years of golf, how could I have such a great swing and be stuck with a nineteen handicap?"

Linc's face was compassionate. "Tell me about the rest of your game."

"I three-putted five greens."

"Is that unusual for you?"

"No, I guess not. To be honest, I haven't put much attention on my putting lately. I'm more concerned with my driving. I really like to hit the ball as far as I can. Usually I'm okay at putting; today, I was terrible. I couldn't get anything in."

"How did you do on the practice green before you went out?"

"Ahh, well, I didn't really have time to practice. They were having the Lotus Club Masters Tournament, at least that's what they called it, and I couldn't resist entering. But I slept late this morning and barely got to the first tee in time to be with my group."

"You didn't tell me you entered a tournament," Linc said, frowning. "I wouldn't normally advise students to do that while they're in the process of learning Quantum Golf. But no matter. Maybe it was necessary in your case," he said, nodding sagely.

"Well, I'll tell you it was no fun having my score posted on that board," Smith complained. "People will think I'm the worst golfer here."

"It seems to me that you recognize quite clearly what happened to you out there."

"Yeah," Smith admitted sheepishly. "I know I shouldn't have rushed to the first tee."

"Quantum Golf starts with your frame of mind, your inner rhythm, a feeling of natural confidence and enjoyment. If you're tense and rush up on the first tee, that tension could stay with you for several holes and ultimately add a considerable number of strokes."

Smith nodded ruefully. He had certainly had *that* experience.

"People who rush from their work to the golf course often find it takes several holes to gain a sense of rhythm. If you're in a time squeeze, or in any way upset by anything, you need to give yourself the gift of slowing down: Take a few moments, sit down quietly, and play a sort of internal movie in which you see yourself swinging in an ideal smooth, fluid, rhythmical motion. *Breathe* yourself into that picture."

"What if you don't have the time to do that?" Smith asked.

"It doesn't take much time. Take a moment now and remember what it feels like to have a good effortless swing."

Smith thought for a few seconds, then nodded.

"Did that take long?" the pro asked.

"Well, no. But is that really going to help?"

"Yes, it will," St. Clair answered. "It will help change your frame of mind. Ideally, you should take considerably longer to warm up before you go out, but if time is short, then you must, at the very least, use your internal movie and take a few swings. You should also make several putts in detail in your mind. In this way, you'll slow yourself down and gain better balance and control. Let me ask you something."

"Yeah?"

"What do you do when you get out of rhythm when you're dancing?"

Smith's face was blank. "Dancing?"

"Yes."

"Oh, dancing!" Smith said. "I don't know"—he smiled—"blame my wife, I guess."

St. Clair raised an eyebrow. "And how does that go over with your wife?"

"Well, actually she often points out other couples who are good dancers."

"That's a very good technique," Linc said. "It's the same in golf. And it really *does* help to watch someone else who is good. You have to stop and pay attention to the rhythm." He removed his hat and hit it against his leg in a pulsing rhythm. "Hear it and feel it in your mind, and then start again in time with the beat. There are always two rhythms that must match; one is internal, and the other is external. Each is affected by the other, so as soon as one changes, the other will respond."

He placed the hat back on his head and went on. "Most golfers aren't even aware of their own internal rhythm, but when we're stressed, agitated, or angry, our internal rhythm speeds up, and this has an effect on the external rhythm. It increases the pace of the swing. We tend to lose our ability to swing smoothly and naturally, and this usually leads to a bad shot. Have you ever noticed that one bad shot often follows another?"

"Yeah, I sure have."

"Even when our mind eventually calms down, we may still continue to swing badly. This is because we lose the smooth connection between the inner and outer rhythms. Our mind-body coordination is temporarily gone. We must stop and *focus* on that smooth, internal rhythm, just as in dancing. It's usually easier to alter the pace of your swing by first altering it in your mind. The inner rhythm is the basis of the outer rhythm."

"I don't know." Smith's gaze wandered over St. Clair's shoulder, past the driving range to the green on the first hole. "I can get pretty upset out there." The green was raised, with steep slopes on either side. "When that happens," he said, "I can tell you, there is no way I'm going to suddenly calm down and think about dancing."

"I understand," St. Clair replied sympathetically. "Let me give you one trick that might help. This is when you probably have the impulse to throw your club."

"Right!"

"Okay. Now, instead of throwing your club, hold it in your hand lightly like this." The teacher held the club between two fingers and let it swing back and forth. He said, "Think of a pendulum swinging, back and forth, back and forth. Do that for a few minutes, allowing your mind to calm down. Relax into that regular smooth pace, that feeling of a perfectly smooth swing. If you're really upset, it may not work immediately, but try it a few times. Let that easy rhythm in your mind match the rhythm of your own golf swing. Let your body mirror your mind. Just hold the fullness of the pendulum image in your mind, and your body will mirror it in an accurate and uncomplicated manner."

"What if your mind is racing so fast you just can't slow it down. I mean, even when you're not particularly upset."

"W-e-l-l . . ." Linc scratched his head, drawing the word out. Smith had a fleeting image of an athletic Will Rogers.

"Some people," St. Clair said, "naturally function at a faster pace than others, so their rhythm might be different. It doesn't matter. The only ideal rhythm is one that is perfectly balanced, perfectly smooth. Never swing your club faster than you swing that pendulum in your mind. Your putting was bad because you were rushing, and your internal rhythm lost its smoothness and flow. Putting is a sensitive thing, like doing brain surgery on a flower." He laughed, delighted with the impossible image. "It can easily be disrupted if you allow yourself to get out of rhythm."

"But it wasn't only my putting that was bad," Smith complained. "My chipping and pitching were horrible, too."

"Tell me about it."

"On the first hole I hit a nice drive with my three wood—not too long, but perfect. Everyone was looking at me and I felt pretty good. Then I hit a five iron. It was a good shot, but I didn't take the strong wind into account so it hit the green, rolled off the edge and down a hill—bad luck really."

"Then what happened?" Linc prompted.

"I took out my sand wedge. I had practiced with it all yesterday after our lesson. I never did have any confidence in the sand wedge before. Well, I thought with Quantum Golf I might try to use it."

"You don't normally pitch with this club?"

"No. For years now I've been using my pitching wedge. One instructor said I handled that club really well. But I know to get close to the hole you really need an accurate sand wedge. All the pros use it. You use a sand wedge for pitching, don't you?"

"Yes, when it's appropriate."

"I got pretty good at the practice green yesterday, but

when I used it the first time in the tournament, I hit the top of the ball hard and it went right over the green." Smith gestured into the distance with his hand.

"I was pretty upset, and I tried to hit it again. This time I made myself keep my head down. That's why I had topped it the first time, y'know. Anyway, I didn't follow through. I just quit in the middle of the swing and it went nowhere. That killed my chance for par, which should have been easy with my first two shots."

Linc was patient. "What happened after that?"

"I missed my putt. I hit way past the hole. And when I putted again I was short. It was the beginning of disaster. I knew this Quantum Golf thing was too good to be true. I'm so frustrated, I could quit."

The pro shook his head and the peacock feather danced in the air. "I have to tell you, Mr. Smith, that what happened today is quite common when people first learn Quantum Golf. Your situation was exaggerated by several things—the pressure of entering a tournament, rushing to the first tee and not taking warm-up putts, as well as using a new club after only one day of practice with it. But really, your underlying problem is simple."

"It is?" Smith clung to Linc's words as if they were a life raft.

"Yes. You haven't yet given up your belief in classical golf. As long as you insist on that viewpoint, it's almost impossible to make the transition to Quantum Golf."

"Impossible?" Smith's raft was sinking. "What do you mean?"

"Take, for example, your pitching and chipping," Linc said. "You told me that after you topped the ball you remembered that you'd lifted your head, right?"

"Yes."

"Thinking about a specific position of your head is a

consideration of classical golf. It's a very good consideration, and one that has to be learned while a person's being trained in the fundamentals of classical golf. But it is not a concern of Quantum Golf."

"It's not?" The life raft was gone, but Smith was still paddling.

"No. Nor is thinking about any other detail of your setup or swing mechanics."

"But I don't see how I can improve my game if I don't pay attention to details," Smith protested. "I mean, that's what an instructor is for—to see what you do wrong and help you correct it."

"That's true of a *classical* instructor," Linc stipulated.

"But don't all pros pay attention to those details? We're always hearing about such and such a pro who's just made an improvement in some aspect of his swing and that's why he's winning the big tournaments."

"Yes, that is what people hear, and it's often true. There are a number of very good classical pros, but they don't win big tournaments playing golf classically."

Smith was now thoroughly at sea. "I don't understand."

"It's entirely possible to have perfect swing mechanics on a classical level. It's also possible to analyze one's swing so that the necessary corrections can be made. But it's not easy. You either have to start golf at a very early age and be well trained, or you spend time hitting thousands of balls under the scrutiny of a top classical instructor. It's a long, tedious process, and in the end, though you may have what appears to be the perfect swing, it's only perfect superficially."

Smith threw his hands in the air. "Now you've really lost me."

"Why, Mr. Smith, there are lots of young pros who

can hit a ball extremely well in friendly situations, but when they try to make the tour they collapse under the pressure. This is because they're relying on a classical swing rather than a Quantum swing. I'm not saying there isn't some element of the quantum in their play, but for all intents and purposes, they are devout believers in the classical system."

Smith spread his hands in question. "So?"

"The point is that their swing is based on a more superficial level, the classical level, and if there's too much pressure on their inner mental state it disrupts their classical swing. No matter how hard they try, they can't maintain enough concentration to deal with the pressures in such intense competition and still hold together all the different aspects of their classical style. They might win one or two tournaments but rarely more than that. These golfers are sometimes called technocrats," Linc said.

"Technocrats?" Smith interrupted. "You mean players who are technically perfect?"

"Yep," Linc replied. "They are very classically precise. For example, they know just how far each of the irons will go. When it comes to feeling and intuition they're often lost, though. Of course, there are intuitive players who play much more from their gut feelings but lack consistency. When they're on, they're really on, but when they're off, they're totally off. What's necessary is a technique that combines the consistency of the technocrats with the feeling level of the intuitive players.

"All really great golfers have put the mechanics on an inner level. Their minds are so well established on this inner level that they're completely confident. They often feel as if they're just watching themselves play golf. It is a paradoxical state, because on the one hand the club head is accelerating very fast, while on the other it seems as if it's in slow motion. It's a very unusual experience, one that is effortless because it's on a deep level."

Smith nodded, following Linc's words intently.

"Whatever small concerns such golfers have about swing mechanics," Linc continued, "are only held lightly in their minds. They're not real concerns, because these golfers know from experience that feeling of an effortless swing. They have confidence in their own inner power. It is the same inner feeling that enables them to make forty-foot putts with ease. Intuitively they know that they're going to make the putt. No doubts can even begin in this state of consciousness. They have seen themselves make it in their mind. And they just do it. Have you ever had this experience?"

"I can't say I've had that feeling very often," Smith said, "but I think I know what you're talking about. I'm a pretty fair public speaker, but when I first started speaking in front of large groups, I got stage fright. After hundreds and hundreds of speeches, I finally got the hang of it, and now my words just flow—I don't even need to prepare. Sure, basically I know what I'm going to say, but I decide on the actual structure or angle of the talk just before the moment. I like to feel out the audience, see who they are, and then it just comes to me—it's almost automatic. Actually, I do seem to watch myself speaking," he said. "And you know what? I use all kinds of words I'd never be able to use in ordinary conversation. While I'm talking and feeling the attention of the audience flowing through me, I'm also standing back and thinking, 'Wow, this is an inspiring lecture. I wonder where it's coming from.' Is this the kind of thing you mean?"

"Yes, precisely. And this brings us to the second fundamental of Quantum Golf. Do you remember the first fundamental?"

"Yes. Frame of mind: You have to change your belief system from the classical to the quantum. I guess I didn't do that very well today, did I?" Smith was downcast.

"It takes a little time. But from what you told me, you've already done it with your three wood and some of your irons."

"Yeah, maybe I have." Smith's face showed that this small taste of success did not satisfy the starving golfer inside him.

"The second fundamental will help you make the transition to Quantum Golf more easily. This second fundamental is called **flow.**"

"Flow? How is that going to help me?"

"Let me use the example of the pendulum again." St. Clair again picked up an iron, holding it easily with two fingers at the extreme end of the club. With wrists and fingers relaxed, he began to gently swing it back and forth.

"You see, this is all there is to the swing, just a rhythmical flow, like a pendulum swinging back and forth. There is change. It moves, it has dynamism, and yet there is also non-change. It constantly and effortlessly repeats itself in a smooth rhythm. It is change and non-change together."

"Hold on, Mr. St. Clair. Now we're talking philosophy, not golf."

"That's true," Linc said, "and the essence of golf *is* more than a game; it's a philosophy of life. In life as well as in golf we must maintain a state of balance between rest and activity. I'll be giving you some specific techniques that will infuse an effortless state of balance into your swing, but first let's understand the nature of balance. The image of the pendulum illustrates useful principles for us. The steady swing of the pendulum illustrates the principle of rest and activity. We begin with rest, then as we draw the club back, we engage in activity. At the top of the backswing there is a moment of rest, or potential activity, and when we begin the downswing, we have activity again. Finally, we finish with rest at the end of the swing. All of life is expressed in cycles of rest and activity. This is a basic rhythm that underlies existence. The quantum world is full of enormous dynamism, full of unlimited energy and infinite frequencies, and yet it is a silent, unchanging world, absolutely quiet and unmanifest."

Smith frowned. "Yeah, well, *I've* never seen such a world."

Linc ignored Smith's growl and, looking at the faraway tree-dotted horizon, continued. "The quantum world contains the most fundamental rhythm from which all other rhythms emerge. In Quantum Golf we make use of that basic rhythm; we allow it to flow effortlessly through our swing, to give us energy. It makes our swing smooth yet dynamic, like the pendulum swinging back and forth."

"So what you mean is that I should be thinking about a pendulum when I swing the club?" Smith queried.

"In essence, yes." Linc turned to him. "You remember how smooth and effortless a pendulum swings?"

"Of course I do." It seemed a simple enough thing to Smith.

"Of course you do!" Linc said. "And this effortless pendulum feeling is just what you experience when you hit your three wood or an iron well. Am I right?" he demanded.

"Yes," Smith admitted. "It's a very smooth motion. It's almost too easy."

"In Quantum Golf that flow is taken to its extreme, it becomes frictionless flow."

"Frictionless . . . you mean like a soap bar sliding in the tub?" Smith asked.

"Yes," replied Linc, pleased with his pupil. "That's a great image. It is something like that, only even more so. You're familiar with the three basic states of matter in physics: solid, liquid, and gas?"

Smith's face was sour. "Now you're talking physics again." He tried by his expression to communicate his dissatisfaction to St. Clair, but the teacher merely returned his gaze with equanimity.

Linc's face seemed to glow with an inner light. Finally Smith admitted, "Yeah, I think I learned that once upon a time."

Linc grinned broadly. "Well," he said, "those three states—solid, liquid, and gas—are not the whole truth, because there is also a fourth state of matter."

Smith frowned darkly. "I've never heard of any fourth state."

"The fourth state is called the superfluid state. An example of a superfluid state occurs when you take liquid helium and cool it to an extremely low temperature, close to absolute zero. This liquid helium undergoes a remarkable transition. It becomes superfluid and starts to display many qualities of the quantum world. Remember I said yesterday that in the quantum world everything is connected?"

"You did?"

Linc nodded and continued, "In its superfluid state, liquid helium reaches a condition of macroscopic quantum coherence."

"Macro what?" Smith squawked. "How can something that sounds like that have anything to do with golf?"

"Macroscopic quantum coherence," Linc repeated

slowly. "Go ahead, just play with the expression; roll it around in your mouth. All it really means is that the liquid helium takes on the characteristics of the quantum world even though it's still a classical system. In other words, frictionless flow, which is a property of the quantum world, exists in everyday life."

"I'm sorry," Smith said stiffly. "I never did very well in school, and this is way over my head. What I want to know is what does all this have to do with lowering my handicap?"

"I'm getting to that," Linc said, and proceeded to confound his pupil further. "The superfluid state is a state in which there is absolutely no friction. Liquid helium will seep through the wall of any container; its flow is perfect. It's almost like a cloud floating, or a mist swirling. It's simply frictionless. All the helium atoms become more closely coupled. Every atom is connected to form a whole that behaves as one. And that, Mr. Smith, is how unified I want your golf swing to be."

Smith's face paled. "Look here, St. Clair," he said. "I'm not a superman. I just want to make par."

The professional regarded him kindly and placed his tanned arm around Smith's shoulder. "It doesn't take a superman to do it. You've already shown me that somewhere among all your different swings is a Quantum swing, and that although you're not able to use it all the time, you have experienced it, so you know what it is. Right?" He tapped Smith expectantly on the back.

Smith agreed hesitantly. "Uh, right."

"Your problem is that you are afraid to let go of the classical world view. It's safe and familiar. The idea of surrendering yourself to the quantum world still terrifies you."

"I don't know about that. I don't think anything has

ever terrified me." St. Clair had challenged Smith's machismo.

"Let me give you a little technique to try while you are playing golf. I think it will make it easier for you."

"Good. I like techniques."

"Before you come up to hit the ball, I want you to say one thing to yourself."

"Keep my head down, right?" Smith guessed with the eager confidence of a good student.

"No, that's a classical technique. What I want you to do is just repeat the words *super fluid*, *super fluid*. At the same time, imagine superfluid helium flowing."

"Blast it, Linc, I don't even know what helium looks like."

"That doesn't matter. Just think of your bar of soap sliding in the tub. It's very slippery, very smooth; there's absolutely no friction."

"I guess I can do that."

"It's the same feeling you naturally have with your three wood. That's because when you go up to hit with it, you have complete confidence. Even if you have classical thoughts about keeping your head down or following through with your swing, they're not as strong as your experience of a real, flowing, effortless swing. You know that no matter what, you're going to hit the ball well because that's just the way you naturally hit your three wood."

Smith was thoughtful. "That's true," he said. "Sometimes I'm so confident with my three wood that just before hitting, for fun I actually try to scare myself with thoughts like, 'You're not going to hit it so well now!' But most of the time it doesn't make any difference what I do. It just works. The silly thing is that I really have no idea why it works. I mean, if I start trying to scare myself before I use my sand wedge, I will top it for sure or hit the ground first."

"With the three wood you're able to function on a quantum level," Linc said happily. "*Because* you're secure and confident with that particular club, your attention isn't fragmented in the details of what makes a good swing. Deep in your inner consciousness the pattern of superfluidity has been established. Your mind knows it and automatically instructs your body in all the complicated movements. You're plugged into your own inner intelligence, a kind of cosmic computer."

Smith nodded. He could imagine such a computer.

Linc went on. "This same cosmic computer is what holds the stars in their places and keeps your heart pumping. The cosmic computer keeps track of all the details. It's just the inner dynamics of nature's intelligence. It allows your swing to unfold in an orderly, fluid flow, in what is virtually a perfectly coordinated sequence of movement. If you tried to remember all the necessary details of your swing, it would only confuse you."

Smith snorted. "I get confused all right. There are so many things to remember." It felt good to finally admit it.

The teacher looked at him mildly. "You aren't successful with your sand wedge because you stay caught in the classical world, trying to remind yourself of all the highly complicated steps in a golf swing—Is my left arm straight? Is my grip too strong? Even if you try to remember only a single detail, it keeps your mind engaged on the classical level and blocks your getting to the deeper quantum level. You have to learn to trust in the quantum level—to let go."

"Sounds good, but just exactly how do I do that?"

"It happens automatically once you have that experience. Once you have had that experience, you've iden-

tified it. Its imprint is on every cell in your body. And it feels so good, so right, that you can't help wanting the experience again. The way you do it is the way you accomplish anything in life—in steps of progress, one step at a time. Don't try to make it happen all at once. Take one step at a time. See everything as a lesson, a chance to grow. Don't worry if the shot is good or bad, only that it's *quantum*, only that it's *effortless* and that you *gain energy* from it."

"What about that superfluid technique you mentioned?" Smith asked. "That bar of soap sliding in the tub?"

"Yes," Linc agreed, "it will help. It will keep your attention off the classical and shift it more toward the quantum. It's only an aid, though, not a substitute for trust in the quantum world view."

"Tell me how it goes again?"

"Before you approach the ball you say the words *super* and *fluid* to yourself."

"*Superfluid*, that's all?"

"That's it, with one addition. You say it to yourself a couple of times as you set up. Now on your backswing, as you take the club back, say 'super' and gently and easily inhale, and then on your downswing and follow-through, gently exhale and say 'fluid.' There should be a distinct gap in time between the two words, coinciding with the moment of rest at the top of your swing, at which time the club appears to almost stop."

"Yeah, I see, to get a kind of rhythm going. I had a teacher once who told me to say 'one' as I brought the club back, and 'two' as I hit the ball."

Linc nodded; the peacock feather on his hat nodded. "The purpose is to establish rhythm, an inner rhythm and an outer rhythm that are coherent. But there are also several other important reasons. One is to put your attention on the wholeness of the swing instead of its parts. And the most important is to evoke in your mind a very delicate feeling, the feeling of **superfluidity**, so that it can permeate from your innermost feeling level to your outermost movements. It is very important to have a good image of superfluidity. What does the word *super* make you think of?"

"Oh, I don't know—something powerful, something extra special."

"Good. Now, what comes to your mind when you think of the word *fluid*?"

"Well, maybe something smooth, like a liquid flowing. Or how about that soap bar slipping in the tub?"

"Good, if that's a clear image for you. Other people may have other images that come to mind—maybe a high-grade oil or something sliding on ice—it doesn't matter. The important thing is have an image that gives the feeling of an effortlessly smooth, dynamic swing. And once you have the experience of it, as you did with your three wood, then you know what it's all about. It's a totally effortless swing that gives you energy. In the beginning I want you to say the words *super* and *fluid* out loud."

"Oh, boy," Smith burst out. "My partners will think I'm crazy. They'll laugh me off the course if they hear me saying stuff like that. I can hear 'em now." His face was glum.

"You can say the words quietly, whisper them," Linc suggested. "When you're more familiar with this technique, then you can stop saying them and just think them. They'll become a part of your swing. And breathing is very important. When you take the club back you must inhale, and when you swing—exhale. If you inhibit your breathing at all, you stop the flow. If you breathe in a gentle, rhythmic manner, then your swing will reflect that rhythm. It's important that it be completely natural and easy. If you can inhale and exhale in an easy manner, then you can swing a golf club in the same effortless manner. Do it a few times and you'll see how easy it is."

Smith inhaled violently, sounding like a broken steam engine. He grew red in the face and felt uncomfortably dizzy. St. Clair put a hand on his arm to steady him.

"Try making your breathing effortless," he suggested. "We shouldn't be able to hear it."

Smith was not used to experiencing much that was effortless. He closed his eyes and huffed and puffed.

"Even softer," Linc suggested. Smith looked at his teacher and gently inhaled a long satisfying breath of clean country air; then he exhaled, relaxing his body completely.

"Again," Linc suggested. Again Smith had a pleasantly relaxing experience of deep, effortless breathing and the attendant relaxation of his mind and body.

"Breathing in this rhythmic manner will also help you do away with any nagging doubts," Linc said. "Saying the words *super* and *fluid* will help take your mind off those classical fears and subtly shift your attention onto the frictionless flow of Quantum Golf."

"Super fluid. That's all I have to say to myself."

"But you can't do it halfheartedly," Linc warned. "You have to really go with the words—*super*, *fluid*—or the result will be that you won't play either good classical golf *or* Quantum Golf." He laughed heartily, evidently finding this idea more amusing than Smith did.

"You must really live superfluidity," he said, "feel that flowing sensation in every part of your body and bones, let it permeate your being. Superfluid, it's just that familiar feeling you have when you hit with your three wood."

Smith made a little face. "Back to the three wood."

Linc nodded. "Your experience with that club is invaluable. It can really help you switch your belief system. It's a kind of stepping-stone that turns on your cosmic computer. But don't force this experience on all your other clubs. The other clubs will naturally be experienced this way when you learn to give up your classical world view with all its fears."

"It doesn't sound like much, just saying *superfluid*."

"When you do it right, it's a whole change in worlds. It's really a very powerful technique."

"I'll give it a try," Smith said halfheartedly.

"It's very important that you give all you have. Don't hedge just because it sounds weird." Linc looked closely at his pupil.

"Okay," Smith promised. "I'll really concentrate on it."

"Don't force it, though. Have fun with it. Your club isn't an instrument of torture. Remember what I said about dancing with the club?"

Smith shrugged. "A little."

"Imagine your club as an extension of yourself, as a dancing partner. You wouldn't grip your partner in a stranglehold or swing her violently around, would you?"

Smith was indignant. "Of course not."

"When you think of 'superfluid,' " Linc said, "think of dancing, think of flowing, guiding your partner gracefully yet purposefully across a dance floor."

"I'll try as hard as I can. I mean . . . I'll try to have fun with it." Smith looked earnest.

"Good. And one more thing: If you happen to forget to dance with your club and swing too hard and the ball doesn't go very far, I don't want you to waste your energy feeling unhappy about it."

"But what if it goes out of bounds or I dub it? I can't just let it go by, can I?"

"Even the best golfers can lose their internal rhythm and miss a shot. The difference between a pro and an amateur is that a pro doesn't usually make two mistakes in a row; he's able to recover quickly after a mistake and *regain his internal rhythm*. The amateur often makes several mistakes in a row. He carries the weight of that first mistake with him, adding to it as he goes. With that burden on his mind and physiology, he can't regain his internal rhythm and keeps making one mistake after another. He has his attention on past errors instead of on his present swing."

"Yeah, but what's a guy supposed to do? I mean, when I get angry, I really get angry." This was a statement Linc could readily believe.

"Every one of us has to learn to deal with some degree of frustration and anger," he said. "There are many different techniques you can use. The one I gave you earlier was for you to take your club lightly in your hand and let it swing back and forth like a pendulum. This can help restore your inner rhythm. The key thing is to turn negativity around to your own advantage. Don't dwell on the mistake. *Don't feed it with energy by putting your attention on it*. What you put your attention on grows stronger in your life. Just treat the mistake with *quiet indifference*. Keep the pendulum swinging smoothly and save your energy for the next shot."

Holding out a stiff, pocket-size printed card to Smith, the pro said, "What I'd like you to focus on now is increasing your number of Q swings. In order to help you succeed, I'm going to give you a Quantum Golf scorecard."

Smith took it in his hand and looked at it. "I don't get it," he said.

"I want you to keep track of each superfluid swing you make," Linc said. "After every swing I want you to mark whether it was an effortless, superfluid Q swing in which you gained energy, or a classical C swing in which you lost energy, regardless of where the ball went. When you finish a round, compute the percentage of superfluid Q swings you had. For example, if you had seventy-five Q swings and twenty-five C swings, your Quantum score would be seventy-five divided by the total number of swings, one hundred."

"You mean seventy-five percent," Smith quickly replied. "Right?"

"Exactly."

"What if I make a swing that's somewhere between a Q and a C swing?"

"Choose whichever it seems closest to. Later you can use an advanced Quantum scorecard, in which you'll make a finer distinction between the two swings."

"The advanced Quantum Golf scorecard . . ." Smith muttered.

"For now I want you only to notice if the swing was classical or quantum, nothing more."

"My Quantum score," Smith repeated, grinning. "Maybe this will be fun. You really don't care what I get?"

"I'm only interested in your percentage of Q swings," Linc assured him. "Your actual golf score makes no difference to me at this point. In fact, it would be best if you thought about your actual score as little as possible."

Smith ground his teeth. "I dunno if I can do that."

"I realize it's difficult," his teacher said, "but you know what happens when you put too much attention on the actual score."

"I know," Smith said. "I get nervous about every shot."

"That's right. Because you're so focused on the score—the result of your action—you forget where the action comes from." He paused. "Have you noticed how some golfers look up, either during their swing or right after, to see where their ball has gone?"

"Yeah, I see it all the time."

"They're more concerned with the results than the swing itself. If the result is good, they're happy and pleased with themselves; if the result is bad, they're angry with themselves. That's why golf can be such an intense, emotional game. Our happiness can be completely attached to a little white ball. A little tiny orb is able to control our mood. We tie ourselves into uncomfortable knots and completely forget we're on a beautiful golf course having an enjoyable day of fun and relaxation."

"I know what you mean," Smith said fervently. "I've had many a day ruined by worrying about where the ball went and what my score was."

"The ball can determine how you feel only if you let it—that is, if you're focused more on the results of the action, your score, than on your own internal rhythm. A good shot comes from a good internal rhythm. By putting your attention on a good internal rhythm you automatically swing the club better and therefore increase your chance of getting a better **Q score.** It's a matter of priorities. By putting your attention on the most important priority, your own internal rhythm, good results follow naturally. And," Linc continued, "you gain energy from each swing rather than putting energy into it. You enjoy the whole game more. It is a *game*, remember?"

Smith scratched at one of his sideburns. "Oh yeah, a game." He grinned.

"One more thing," Linc added. "To make it easier for you to keep your attention on your internal rhythm, for the time being I want you to limit yourself to using only those clubs you feel the most comfortable with. If there's a club that's difficult for you—your sand wedge, for instance—don't use it. Later on you can work with those clubs at a driving range."

"What if I get in a sand trap?" A vision of himself as an ant at the bottom of a mountain of sand entered Smith's mind.

"Do you have trouble with your sand wedge in traps?" Linc asked. "I thought it was only in pitching."

"Well,"—Smith's face wobbled as the mountain of sand diminished somewhat for the valiant ant—"that's true, I guess."

"I'm not trying to deprive you of your clubs," the teacher reassured him. "They're all very important. But you have to learn to walk before you can run. I want to get your swing flowing, and any anticipation or worry about a particular club will disturb that flow. It's like a young, growing seedling—you must be delicate with it, nurture it, get it strong before you use it to build your house."

"A young seedling. Yeah," Smith said, "that's what I am." As he spoke, Smith's experience-lined face actually took on a youthful air.

Linc nodded gravely, the peacock feather bobbing in accompaniment. "You are about to enter a new universe. It's important to put aside all your hard-driving worldly business experience. In this new world, you're still a child and there is a lot to learn. You must treat yourself with respect and humility. Be serious and yet joyful. Don't try to impress your friends or anyone else." His voice softened. "You're like a child in the quantum world, and it's natural for a child to make so-called mistakes as he learns. If a child gets up and falls, that's okay; it's part of learning. But if the child just lies down and never even tries to get up, then there is no opportunity to learn. There is nothing to be ashamed of. Just enjoy

experiencing the flow of superfluidity. Dance with the club."

Smith looked at Linc with something close to reverence. For the first time in years he felt a simple side of himself, an innocence that he didn't even remember feeling as a child. His eyes followed his mentor as the teacher saluted him and strode away.

Practice Drills for Chapter 2

1. Practice the **Superfluid Routine**. This routine consists of:

(a) Lightly hold the club between your fingers. Let it swing like a pendulum. Notice how easily and effortlessly it swings and how fast the club head moves. Now grip the club hard with your hand and let it swing, notice how the club head slows down. Go back to gripping it lightly and again notice how effortlessly the pendulum swings. *Do less and accomplish more.*

(b) Every time the club swings back say the word *super* and at the same time gently and easily *inhale*. Repeat this several times as the club continues to swing back and forth in your fingers. Now, as the club swings forward, say the word *fluid* and *exhale*. Try to exhale fully. Accommodate your breathing to your swing so that you don't have any air left at the end of the swing. Experiment with the pace of your breathing, see how much air you require, find what feels most natural.

Repeat this several times saying the word *super* and inhaling as the club swings back in your fingers and saying the word *fluid* and exhaling as the club swings forward. Notice the moment when the club appears to stop at the top of the backswing and at the top of the forward swing. This moment of rest is an important moment of potential activity. There should be a distinct gap in time between the words *super* and *fluid*, which coincides with that moment of rest. This gap should also exist in your normal swing during a game. It's from here, from the gap, that the club accelerates. Without this gap the smooth rhythm and potential power of the superfluid swing is lost.

(c) Keep the image and feeling of the superfluid pendulum alive as you set up to make your swing. Now on the backswing, as you take your club back say "super" and gently and easily *inhale*, and then on your downswing and follow-through, gently *exhale* and say "fluid." Say the words quietly at first and then later just think the words.

2. Practice swinging and hitting the ball with a lofted club (like a seven or eight iron) with your feet together. If you lose your balance then you're swinging too hard, using too much effort. Swing more lightly until it's easy to keep your balance. This will improve your balance and take you toward a more effortless swing.

3. Continue to swing with your feet together, only this time also use the Quantum practice grip. In the Quantum practice grip you start by taking a normal grip, then slide the fingers of your right hand so they completely overlap the fingers of the left hand. Don't grip too hard with your left hand. Use no effort, be light. Feel light in your take-away, the first moment of the backswing, and the whole swing will be light.

It may seem awkward at first, but never mind; just swing without worrying where the ball goes.

4. To make a **Quantum scorecard**, take a normal scorecard and for each hole use the vertical column to mark whether your swings were superfluid Q swings or classical C swings. When you finish the round, compute the percentage of superfluid Q swings to get your Q score. Bring along a notebook and write down experiences or thoughts about your Quantum swing.

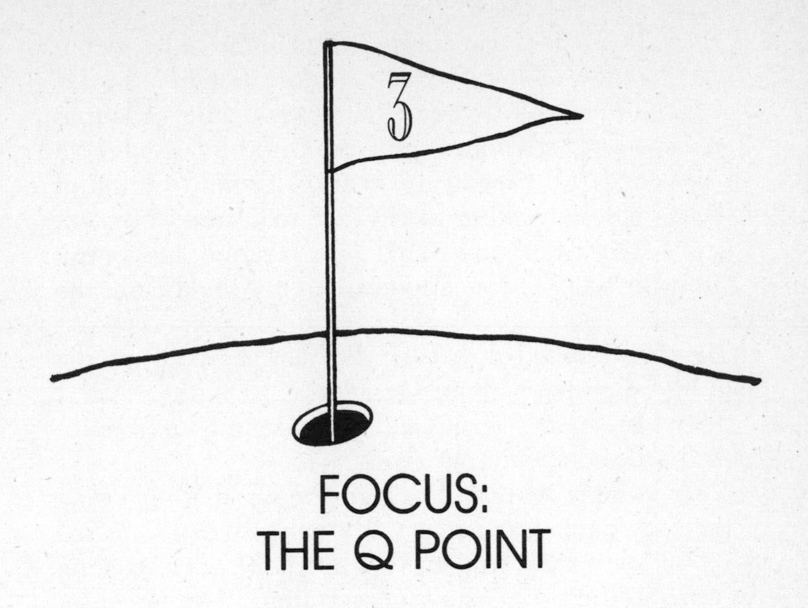

FOCUS: THE Q POINT

Humming a Strauss waltz, Smith used a flashlight to steer a path through the dark rose garden. Whippoorwills sang and fireflies glowed intermittently. Only a day after his ignominious showing at the Lotus Golf Tournament, he'd played a great round of golf and followed that up with a wonderful dinner at the clubhouse. Yessiree, all was right with the world. He was inhaling the scented night air when he heard the soft thump of a putter hitting a ball, and a moment later the plunk of it hitting the backside of the cup. Who could be out there playing in the blackness of the night?

Linc's now familiar voice inquired out of the dark, "How was your swing today, Mr. Smith?"

"Oh, there you are," Smith said, flashing his light in his teacher's direction. He stood, watching him make the putt. "I tried to find you today, but they told me you were at the farm."

"Yes," Linc said, chuckling. "One of the bulls got out this afternoon and was terrorizing the neighborhood." He shook his head. "If they'd only known he's about as fierce as a kitten. The real problem with him is that he'd sit in your lap if he had the chance. Come to think of it," he said, scratching his head, "that could be a bit scary." They both laughed. Linc tapped his putter against the ball. They could hear but not see it enter the cup.

Smith wondered how Linc did that, how he hit the ball into the hole without seeing it.

"So, Mr. Smith," Linc said, straightening up from his putt, "tell me about your swing."

"My swing? Oh, *that.* I'm happy to say that my swing today was darn near perfect. I was consistent, not too long but extremely straight. It was a little nerve-racking to tell you the truth," he said, grinning. "I've never hit so many straight balls."

"How was your Quantum score?"

"Leaving out the putts?"

"Yes, for now. We'll consider putting in the next lesson."

"Then my Quantum score was seventy-five percent."

St. Clair playfully patted Smith on the back in congratulation. "That's pretty high," he said, and asked, "Did you feel good about it?"

"Yes and no," Smith responded. "I was absolutely amazed at how easy and consistent my swing was. I kept saying to myself, 'This can't go on, I've got to make a mistake soon.' There were a few times, though, when I lost my concentration and made mistakes."

Linc said thoughtfully, "You shouldn't direct your attention to mistakes; only be concerned about your superfluid swings, the swings you *gain* energy from." His eyebrows rose lightly as he said, "What you direct your attention to grows in your life."

"Yes." Smith regarded him with intensity. "That makes sense," he said, "but I was nervous. I mean, you said I should get energy from each swing, only it wasn't quite like that. I kept feeling that my success wasn't going to last. I thought, at any minute now I'm going to blow it."

"When you did have a good swing, what exactly did you feel?"

"My arms were so light and my swing was so effortless, it felt automatic. I guess I had to restrain myself quite a bit, since I normally love to kill the ball."

"Let me put you at ease, Mr. Smith. You did very well indeed."

"I did?"

"Yes, you made a great step forward today, and I know it wasn't easy for you."

Smith spoke ponderously, "No, it wasn't easy." He looked down at his feet, his mind a battlefield between classical and quantum.

"It's natural that you'd feel uncomfortable," St. Clair explained. "Successful Quantum Golf is very different from what you've been playing for the last five years."

Smith agreed. "Very different."

"I'm proud of you, Mr. Smith. In spite of your desire to kill the ball, you restrained yourself and the result was that you were able to have a Quantum swing. The fact that you didn't hit the ball far is fine; in fact, it's excellent."

"It is?"

"Yes, you're still on the threshold of the quantum mechanical world; that's why you felt strain instead of energy, that's why the ball didn't go as far. A true Quantum swing will give you energy, as I said, and it goes very far. But that takes some time to acquire—not too long, but some time of practice."

"How long? I want to hit farther now," Smith said fiercely, the beam from his gesturing flashlight flailing wild paths against the dark sky.

"And you will," Linc soothed him, "you will, but first we must establish the flow of the swing. Our lesson yesterday was superfluid flow. And you felt that superfluid flow, didn't you?"

"I did," Smith said excitedly. "It was an incredible feeling of ease. I couldn't get over how little effort I put into each swing. I really did feel the superfluid flow."

"It will become more and more superfluid with time," Linc said. "But for your next month of playing I just want you to keep at this same easy level. Please don't try to hit the ball far," he cautioned. "If you're worried that with an easier swing the ball won't go as far, then use a less-lofted club—for example, a four iron instead of a five. Distance and score are not important now. The important thing is to keep feeling that superfluid flow. You have to be very strict with yourself. When you play with old rivals you'll be tempted to hit the ball hard in order to hit as far as they do, but you must discipline yourself." The teacher's eyes were sparks of sternness in the dark. "Do you agree?"

Smith was not happy. His flashlight wavered toward the ground. "I guess so," he replied.

"I don't want a tentative answer, I want a firm commitment," the pro demanded.

"All right. I'll try my hardest. But what if they start kidding me about how short my drives are?"

"Don't pay attention to anyone else. Direct your attention to yourself, to your own game."

"How do I do that?"

"Through **focus**. That is our lesson for today," Linc said, "focus. It has to do with the particle and the field."

"The particle and the field? You've lost me again."

Linc paused a moment before answering. "I told you that in classical physics the world was believed to be made of particles—solid atoms of matter, the basic building blocks of the universe."

"Yeah, I got that."

"In quantum physics, the particle is no longer solid. It's just a bump or wave in a field. The field is the primary reality; it is everything and everywhere, an infinite field underlying all diversity."

"An infinite what?"

"An infinite state. An unbounded, unmanifest, and perfectly orderly unified state, a unified field connecting everything."

Smith scowled into the blackness. "What does all this have to do with focusing during my golf swing?"

"Everything," Linc said, and continued, "You mentioned that sometimes when you're about to swing, a little voice inside you says you're going to make a mistake."

"Yeah," Smith agreed. "It happens all the time."

"It's like an internal dialogue with yourself," Linc suggested. "Yourself talking to yourself, right?"

"That's it exactly. It drives me crazy."

"That's your small self talking," Linc said, "the one that always worries about everything. The small self is like a wave and the big Self is the ocean. One is the part and the other is the whole. A physicist would say that the small self is like the particle, and the big Self is like the field."

"Sometimes I just can't get what you're saying." Smith

was desperate for illumination. "I have a hard enough time when you're talking plain golf. All I want to do is lower my score!"

"You'll do it," Linc assured him. "I'll explain the concept more fully. Your small self is the voice inside you that keeps up an incessant dialogue: nagging, criticizing, humiliating, praising, bragging. Because it's small it can often be full of fears and worries, especially when you're about to do something that can be judged by others, such as swinging a golf club. This small self mainly focuses on details, but in the case of a golf swing, you know that too much focus on the details of the swing can lead to a classical attitude, which is an easy prey to mistakes. If the small self is busy analyzing, a kind of duality between the mind and feelings is created."

"Duality?" Smith asked in confusion.

"For instance, as you putt, the mind says, 'It's going to be a straight putt,' but at the last moment your feeling tells you the ball is going to curve to the left. This creates duality; you start to doubt the stroke. Doubts create fear. Fear leads to restrictions on your swing. You're afraid of making a mistake and losing your rhythm. The mind gets confused. The mind is so busy worrying and doubting that it stops sending the correct signals to swing the club smoothly. The result is that you make all kinds of mistakes. In the extreme it can lead to the 'yips,' where even the best pro can't make an easy putt."

"I've heard about the yips . . . sounds terrible. How they missed me I'll never know."

"The yips is a terrible phenomenon," the teacher agreed. "The mind becomes so tense that it ties the muscles in knots. All smoothness is gone, replaced by a jerky, spasmodic swing." He paused. "It's the ultimate confusion created by a duality between mind and feelings."

"Aha," Smith said slowly. "I can see that, but how can I *control* my small self? I mean, what if I have an unconscious thought that I have *got* to hit the ball hard?"

Linc laughed softly. "It's very difficult," he said, "to totally eliminate your small self, but you can sometimes trick it by saying the words *super* and *fluid* when you swing."

"How does that trick the small self?"

"It gets so caught up in repeating '*superfluid*' and actually producing a taste of the experience of superfluidity that it forgets to introduce doubts into your swing. The fears and worries are still there, but for a brief moment they are in the background. But the small self is smart. It can't be tricked forever. Sooner or later it begins to catch on."

"Yes," Smith spoke eagerly, "I had the experience on the second nine. That little voice inside me told me several times that it was too good to be true and that I'd make a mistake, and once or twice I did make a mistake. But you know, by that time I'd gained so much confidence in my superfluid swing that I could get that little voice to cooperate and get it to feel the *superfluid* feeling."

"That's great." Linc was proud of his student. His eyes shone in the beam of Smith's flashlight. "You began to doubt the doubt," he said. "Do you know why that is?"

"Why?"

"Because when you had that superfluid feeling, that sense of confidence in your swing being just right, then your small self started to *expand*."

Smith was puzzled. "I don't get it."

"When you become confident," Linc explained, "your small self expands. It becomes less doubting, less afraid. It's impossible to eliminate the small self, but what we can do is *expand* it into the big Self. It's like a king with a small territory and very few warriors. He must build high walls"—he gestured with his hands—"and be constantly vigilant against invaders. However, if his territory expands and he has many large castles and many great knights to fight for him, he can feel confident. He can relax. He does not fear being overpowered and destroyed."

"So," Smith responded, getting into the idea, "when I started to feel confidence in my superfluid swing, my small self began to expand and became stronger."

"Exactly," Linc said. His face appeared brighter and brighter in the flashlight's beam. "The superfluid feeling takes the small self to the quantum mechanical level of your life, the quantum field. And you become your 'big Self.' You are in essence the field, rather than the particle."

"I sort of understand," Smith said. "I *feel* what you are saying is right, but it still sounds pretty abstract." What was going on? Linc looked like he was being illuminated with Klieg lights. Maybe, Smith thought, I got too much sun today. He mentally reviewed his evening meal at the club, but decided he'd neither ingested nor drunk anything that might result in such a hallucination. Whatever was going on, it darn well wasn't *him*.

Linc's voice interrupted his ruminations. "It's actually very concrete," Linc told him. "It's the reality of life, and it will be more and more real to you in time. In our last lesson I'll tell you about a practical technique that'll give you a way to regularly expand your small self. For now, all you have to do is recognize that dominant feeling of confidence in which classical fears can still be present but are in the background."

"Yeah," Smith agreed. "I remember that sensation."

"Okay," Linc said. "Now let's explore focusing a bit more." He motioned his pupil toward the practice range.

Feeling he no longer needed the flashlight, Smith shoved it into his pocket and followed the pro through the yew hedge to the range.

"Having established an inner superfluid rhythm, we've created a foundation for your swing, and on the basis of that foundation we can now make some important improvements."

"Will these improvements help my distance?" Smith asked. There was not much in life that could distract him for long from his dearest wish, to hit a golf ball long and far.

"Yes, merely by adding one more simple technique, both your distance and accuracy should improve markedly."

There was a long pause. Smith looked expectantly at his teacher. Finally he could contain himself no longer. He burst forth, "Well, what is it?"

"It is called the **Q point**."

"What's a Q point?" Smith's eyes narrowed in suspicion.

"The Q point is the final position of an effortless swing." Linc held a seven iron out to Smith, "Here, take this and hit some balls."

Smith was incredulous. "In the dark?"

"Sure," his teacher said easily. "It's the same club, same ball. Try it."

Reluctantly, Smith took the club from St. Clair's hand and hit a few balls. He remembered to inhale the word *super* on his backswing, and exhale the word *fluid* on his downstroke.

On his third try he made a perfectly effortless swing. The ball rose and for a moment hung white and ghostly against the night sky. At the end of Smith's swing Linc called out, "Hold that final position."

Smith froze at the final point of his swing. "What do I do now?" he called over his shoulder.

Linc walked up to him. "I want you to see where your arms and hands are."

Smith turned his neck awkwardly, looking back over his left shoulder in an attempt to regard his arms and hands without breaking the pose.

"Now let me help you feel this position," Linc said. Smith rigidly maintained his posture.

"Please, Mr. Smith, relax a little."

"I *am* relaxed," Smith countered through clenched teeth. The flashlight bulged uncomfortably into his thigh.

"Take a deep breath, please."

Smith breathed in and out, his muscles losing their tension with his exhalation. He felt better, and the pose felt right.

"Excellent," Linc said. "This is your Q point, the final position your golf swing should always arrive at. You have succeeded in creating a very nice inner rhythm in your swing, but there is still a tendency for you not to follow through completely. A strong image of this Q point will help you swing *through* the ball rather than swing at it."

"How long do I have to stay like this?" Smith asked.

"Take your time to really notice where your arms are; notice what your left hand feels like, how your back feels, where your feet are, especially your right foot, what angle your head is at, and how you are breathing. Make a mental movie of everything about your perfect Q point. Make it in living technicolor, or"—Linc grinned into the darkness—"in black and white."

Smith did not feel in a position to appreciate any jokes and after a minute or two he cried out, "I can't stay like this forever!"

"Do you have a clear, precise image of what your Q point is?"

"Yes, yes," Smith said. "Very clear."

"Is it comfortable?"

"Whadda you think? It may have been comfortable at first . . . I don't know anymore. I feel like I'm on another planet. Do I have to stay like this all night?"

The teacher laughed. "No, you can relax."

Smith's breath came out in a deep sigh as his arms flopped to his side.

"Take a few more practice swings and see if you can reach your perfect Q point again. Remember to exhale all the way to your Q point."

Smith took several practice swings, holding and adjusting his final position at the end of the swing until Linc agreed that he had indeed reached his Q point.

"All right. Now, before every shot on any golf course, I want you to step back from the ball and first take a practice swing, holding your Q point position for a few moments. Then when you come up to the ball to actually hit it, have the *faint intention* of reaching that Q point, and hold in your mind all the sensations of that experience. Once that image is clear for you, then let go completely," he said. "*Forget it.* Take your normal stance and go back to your superfluid flow technique as in any other swing."

"But what if I keep having the image of the Q point?"

"Then let it be there, but don't put any attention on it. Your concern when you swing should only be on saying 'super' as you inhale with your backswing—"

"I know, and 'fluid' as I exhale on my downswing." Smith sighed heavily. It had been a long evening.

"One more thing," Linc continued. "Whenever you're chipping or pitching, you should also use the image of the Q point. The placement of your Q point will vary depending on whether you take a three-quarter swing or a half swing. I don't want you to be concerned whether the ball went far or short, only whether you reached the Q point you'd decided upon before the shot."

Smith felt vague panic. "How do I know what it will be for each shot?"

"Especially when you chip, you must *decide ahead of time how much of a swing you need*. To be fair to yourself, you should go to a practice green—take a seven iron, for example—and test just how far the ball goes when you finish your swing at three-quarters of full follow-through, at half, and so forth." In a voice full of energy and enthusiasm, Linc suggested, "Try a few chips right now."

"It might be easier to do this during the day," Smith remarked.

"There isn't enough light for you?" Linc asked.

Smith was relieved the pro had brought up the subject of light. He didn't want to believe it was his imagination. "Actually," he said, "it's pretty bright."

The landscape was strangely illuminated as if by day.

"Do they have some kind of northern lights phenomenon here?" Smith asked. St. Clair laughed softly but didn't respond to the question.

"Maybe," the teacher said, "it would be better if you practiced your Q point tomorrow. And remember, just before you swing, to focus attention only on your inner rhythm—on the superfluid flow. This will ensure that you have the feeling of being simultaneously both the particle and the field, of both a sharp focus and a broad comprehension. You'll never lose sight of the forest even though you're looking at a particular tree. Just have the faint intention of a specific goal—your Q point—and then let it go and step into the superfluid flow of your swing."

Smith found Linc's face so bright now that he had to

look slightly away as he asked his fondest question: "Do you really think I'll be able to hit the ball farther with this technique?"

"Yes, effortlessly and automatically it will go quite a bit farther, without any real trying on your part. These techniques will take your attention from the part to the whole and finally to your big Self. Remember the cosmic computer?"

Smith nodded. "Sure."

"The cosmic computer is nature's intelligence. It's inside everything in nature, including yourself. It is, in fact, the big Self. We are so caught up in our small selves that we are often unaware that it exists. Only occasionally are we able to relax and tap into it. In those moments though, we can feel it automatically and experience its infinite, computational power. Whatever we're doing—playing basketball, dancing, public speaking, skiing, surfing, sailing—giving ourselves up to the cosmic computer allows us to do things better, beyond better."

"I've had that experience sometimes," Smith said.

"It's not a totally unfamiliar thing," Linc said. "Everyone has had some experience of it, especially great athletes. They often talk about being in the groove, in the flow, in the zone. These are times when they can't seem to miss. Their cosmic computer takes literally everything into account, and does it perfectly. It takes all the many factors in your golf swing: your grip, your backswing, your weight shift, and computes and coordinates everything exactly and ideally. When you're connected to the cosmic computer, you're on automatic pilot. Nature takes care of everything for you."

"Sounds pretty good." The universe seemed good to Smith, and he looked around in appreciation at his surroundings, which were unusually bright at that moment.

"Yes, it has a great feeling to it," Linc said, his blue

eyes brilliant. "It's a feeling full of power and joy of the mastery of life. It's really very wonderful. One thing though."

"What's that?" Smith asked.

"It has to be natural. It has to come from *inside* ourselves. It can't be imposed or faked in any way, especially if we are very tired or stressed."

"Why is that?"

"Because it really is the flow of nature's intelligence. If we make a mood of it, then we'll be forcing and that will only stop the flow. And if we're too tired or stressed, that can also stop the flow."

"But," Smith protested, "I've played some of my best matches after a good party."

"Do you find this is always true?"

Smith realized he was being ridiculous. "No," he admitted, "but I remember doing it once or twice. If I'm very tired, I usually flub."

Linc nodded. "There are always exceptions. It's possible that when we're very tired we stop caring about the results of the game and about our score. In a mood of what could almost be called detachment we're able to let go, stop focusing on results, and we are able to take an easy swing. But it's a highly unreliable and negative approach."

"Yes," Smith agreed, "I can see that." His now useless flashlight dropped unnoticed from his pocket to the grass below.

"What we want in golf is to have a way to be permanently connected to the cosmic computer."

Smith didn't care where the light around them emanated from. He felt warmed and enlivened by its glow. Then he realized what he had been thinking and mopped his brow. He must be more tired than he'd realized.

Linc was saying, ". . . In order to do this we must

have both a clear mental state and a properly functioning body. If we compare ourselves to a computer, then we can think of our consciousness, our thoughts, as the software and our brain as the hardware. Normally our software and hardware are not being used to their full potential. But the clearer our thinking, the better our software; the more rested and healthy our bodies, the better our hardware. To be connected to the cosmic computer, to be connected to our big Self, both our software and hardware have to be working well, and they have to be compatible."

Whatever doubts Smith had about his own hardware, he was certainly in awe of Linc's.

"There are moments," St. Clair said, "when our software and hardware become simultaneously upgraded and we're connected to the internal rhythm of nature. Everything seems to go just right. Our swing, for example, is perfect at those moments. At that time we're using the full power of the cosmic computer. Our software and hardware actually become that of the cosmic computer. Every single thing is spontaneously computed for us. And once we have complete confidence in the experience, our swing becomes superfluid, and golf becomes totally effortless and enjoyable."

Linc turned to leave. "Just remember, it's easy to connect ourselves to the cosmic computer, and in this way we become superfluid."

Smith followed what seemed to be a trail of light. His gruff voice echoed in the night as he whispered to himself, "Superfluid, superfluid, superfluid."

Practice Drills for Chapter 3

1. Swing the club without a ball and practice getting to your **Q point**. Have a good instructor verify that you're at the right Q point. Notice how your arms feel, the position of your hands. Are you upright? Is your back arched? Are you still breathing easily? What is the position and weight of your feet? Do this a number of times so that you have a clear feeling and image of your Q point.

2. At the driving range take out a seven iron. Before each shot step back from the ball and take a practice swing, holding your Q point position for a few moments and remembering the feel of it. Now step up to the ball. Have only the faint intention of reaching that Q point. Once that image is clear for you, then let go of it completely, forget it. Take your normal stance and go back to your superfluid flow technique as in any other swing.

3. Go to a practice green and take a seven iron. Test just how far the ball goes when your Q point ends at a quarter swing, a half swing, and so forth. Now try another club and do the same thing until you have a feel for how far the ball will roll for each Q point position.

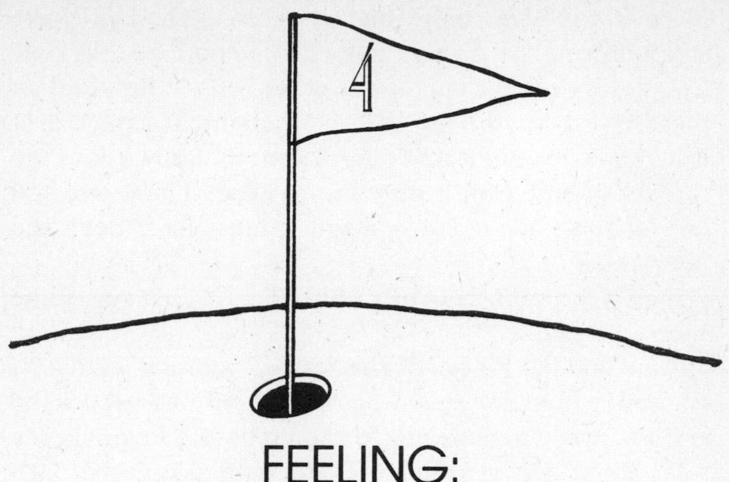

FEELING: QUANTUM VISION

Smith parked his golf cart on a paved area beside the driving range. He lifted his clubs from the back of his cart and, rather than go along the shell path, he jumped athletically over the low white rope that marked off the practice area. Under a vast Iowa sky, his teacher was hitting balls. Linc was about to take a shot. His evidently everpresent straw hat was set firmly on his brow, the peacock feather iridescent in the sunlight.

What kind of practice was this anyway? If Smith's eyes weren't deceiving him, St. Clair had . . . not one ball on the tee, but *three* balls. Yes! he had three balls, one balanced on top of the other, all perching upon the tee.

And Linc's club was turned around! Its face was completely reversed as Smith watched the pro draw it back for a stroke. The club sailed through all three balls like a hot knife through butter. One ball rocketed on a low trajectory that went past the 200-yard mark. It was the most bizarre shot Smith had ever seen. His eyes were still following the distant ball when he noticed that Linc had already caught one of the other balls in his hand. It must have been the top ball, he thought. It looked as if it had flown straight up from the tee and down into the teacher's hand. Smith stared at the tee. There was still one ball left on it. He realized it must have been the bottom ball.

Slowly he walked over to St. Clair. "That was some shot," he said.

Linc nodded his head, the feather bobbing wildly. "I learned it from a wily old Scotsman, only he used to do it with a wooden club and feathered balls. He taught me a lot about golf . . . and life," he added quietly. "It's nothing special; lots of pros can do it. But I like to do unusual shots every so often." He smiled shyly. "It reminds me that golf really *is* a game and that what we are doing is playing."

"But the club face was reversed!"

Linc shrugged. "Yes. Well, you never know when you might find your ball under a bush or on the other side of a tree. I like interesting lies, don't you?"

His student was silent, his lips pressed in a thin line. Interesting lies indeed, Smith thought. *He* considered it a personal affront of nature if he found his ball on anything but the softest bed of green grass.

"How was your score today?" Linc asked.

Smith beamed at him, speaking through a widely stretched smile, "I got an eighty-one, my best ever."

"No, I mean your **Q score**."

Suddenly crestfallen, Smith said, "Oh that. My Q score was pretty good—eighty-five percent. But I still made a few mistakes," he admitted, adding quickly, "I suppose I wasn't completely superfluid."

"I see," St. Clair was thoughtful. "How was your Q point?"

"Hey, I want to tell you, that's some trick. I hit the ball fifteen to twenty yards farther on my drives and ten yards farther on the irons." Smith was beaming again.

Linc tilted the hat back on his head. He grinned at his pupil and said, "Wonderful, Mr. Smith. I know how much that means to you."

Smith's face, his whole body, looked much more relaxed and at ease than three days ago. "My putting was even better." His eyes flickered up to Linc's hat, where the peacock feather still sprang jauntily from the band. Maybe he should think about getting a hat like that—just to wear in Iowa, of course.

"What was it about your putting that was better?" Linc asked.

"I had that good superfluid feeling in my putting. I guess that doesn't explain much."

"No," Linc said. "It explains everything." He stood with his tanned arms crossed over his chest, biceps delineated against his thin cotton shirt.

"It does?" Smith's eyebrows rose above his eyes, which today were as clear as a young athlete's.

"Yes." Linc unfolded his arms and stepped nearer to Smith. "**Feeling** is the subject of today's lesson. **Feeling** is a deeper way of experiencing flow. In the past three lessons we've been speaking mostly about the mechanical or physical experience of superfluid flow. Now I want you to go to a deeper level and experience a more abstract and subtle feeling of flow."

"Yeah, I'd like that," Smith said happily.

"Our first priority is the feeling of superfluidity. It is only on the basis of this feeling that we can improve our swing. When you build a house you first have a blueprint of the whole plan. Each room must have its context in relation to the whole. It's the same in golf. Without the inner rhythm being established, without the wholeness of superfluidity in the swing, it's very difficult to correct any single aspect of the swing."

"Hmmm." Smith thought about it. "I can't understand why I've been struggling so much. I've been obsessed with trying to be a better golfer. Last year I went to the driving range every day, and I must have taken thirty private lessons. The whole thing was terribly frustrating."

"It was frustrating," Linc said, "because you were trying to perfect your swing on the classical level. Many golfers believe that only when their swing is technically perfect can they play well and be an ideal player. They try systemically to improve each part of their swing, first to get the backswing perfect, the turning of the shoulders, and so forth. Doing it this way can take years. In trying to get a perfect swing on the classical level they set a goal for themselves that they'll almost certainly fail to achieve most of the time."

"What is the perfect swing anyway?"

"There are quite a few top pros who have what people consider to be a perfect swing, but each of their swings is different. What is perfect for one person's body, temperament, and character could be disastrous for someone else. The perfect swing is uniquely and intimately related to the individual. The problem is that every golfer is different from every other golfer. Each has a slightly different grip pressure, posture, stance, et cetera. Therefore every swing looks a little bit different. I believe that the most important common denominator among top pros who naturally have a superfluid swing is what we can't see—they *gain energy* from their swing."

"You've talked about that before," Smith remarked, "but there are good classical golfers who win tournaments, aren't there?"

"Yes, but those are the classical golfers who are able to relax automatically to that feeling level before they swing. The whole process has been so deeply programmed into their muscles that their minds can rest. They momentarily stop analyzing and allow their cosmic computer to take over. Unfortunately, because they still deeply believe in the classical system, the moment they make any kind of mistake they revert back to a classical swing, and this disconnects them from the cosmic computer."

Smith nodded thoughtfully. "I think the whole thing is becoming a lot clearer to me, both as a result of your explanation and of my own experience these last few days." He spoke earnestly. "I've begun to switch my belief system. I think I can honestly say I am a believer in Quantum Golf."

"Very good," Linc said. "That's all it takes, an initial commitment, and then the experience is self-reinforcing. Once you've experienced the Q swing," he said, grinning, "it's so easy and feels so delightful that you naturally want more and more of it. I have a few simple exercises for you to help develop your level of feeling."

Smith was ready for anything. "More techniques, huh?"

"Right," Linc said, smiling. "First, the most important way to sense your level of feeling is in putting. Many people don't emphasize putting, but it's really the most important part of the game. Of course, all aspects of the game are important, but there's a saying on the tour: Drive for show and putt for dough. Putting is what distinguishes one pro from another. There are a lot of pros who can hit a long ball, but there are only a handful who can make repeated thirty-foot putts in a championship match with a large crowd watching. There is enormous pressure and excitement at those moments, and it's absolutely vital that the golfer be completely grounded in a very deep level of feeling and remain in the big Self."

Smith was insistent. "How do you do that?"

"All the different techniques I've been giving you have helped increase your experience of the feeling of a superfluid swing."

Smith agreed.

"And the techniques I gave you for focusing—thinking about your Q point—helps to establish the image of a complete superfluid swing on the feeling level."

"Yeah," Smith said, remembering his game earlier. He nodded. "Those techniques really worked for me."

"Good. Today I'm going to give you another technique. It's called **Q vision.**"

"I'm getting to like this Q stuff."

"Q vision is not the ordinary way of seeing things. The most important things in life we can't see with our eyes. We have to learn to use our heart."

"My heart?" Smith's eyes bulged, then he frowned. "This I've got to see."

"You'll see," Linc said confidently. "Q vision starts with your eyes. It works like this: When you step behind the ball, you pick out a target and look at where you want the ball to land—for instance, a small patch of ground on the fairway or a spot on the green. You make sure that the target is within eighty percent of your normal distance capacity, not more. This will ensure a *confident*, effortless swing."

He looked at Smith, who was clearly absorbing every word, and continued, "Your superfluid swing should lead you to something. It's like driving a car. You want a smooth ride, but you also want to go someplace. Hitting as far as possible is no target. It will tense your muscles. It will make it more difficult for you to be superfluid in your swing. It's like passing a basketball—you want it to go from person A to person B, not from person A to as far as possible. If you're shooting to the green or near the green, pick a spot there. Is this clear?"

"I think so. I imagine a spot where I want the ball to go."

"Good."

Smith harrumphed. "Seems to me that it takes more than imagination and good feeling to get the ball there!"

"You'll be surprised. If you don't give your mind a clear vision of what you want the body to do, it won't be able to do it."

"That I can understand."

"All right. Now, once you have a very clear image of what you want to do, then you simply let it go, forget it."

"Really, St. Clair," Smith said, annoyed, "one minute you want me to imagine something and the next minute to forget it. Where's the logic?"

"There's a very deep logic to it. You see, if you try too hard to keep an image in your mind, then your small self takes over, analyzing, criticizing and in general making a mess of things. It's the same procedure you used with the Q point. You had the intention to swing the club to a certain point, and then you forgot it and went back to the inner rhythm of your superfluid swing. It worked when you did it then, didn't it?"

"Why yes, it did."

"In Q vision you do the same thing, only now you're extending your intention to include exactly where you want the ball to go."

"What about this seeing with the heart thing? You were kidding about that, right?"

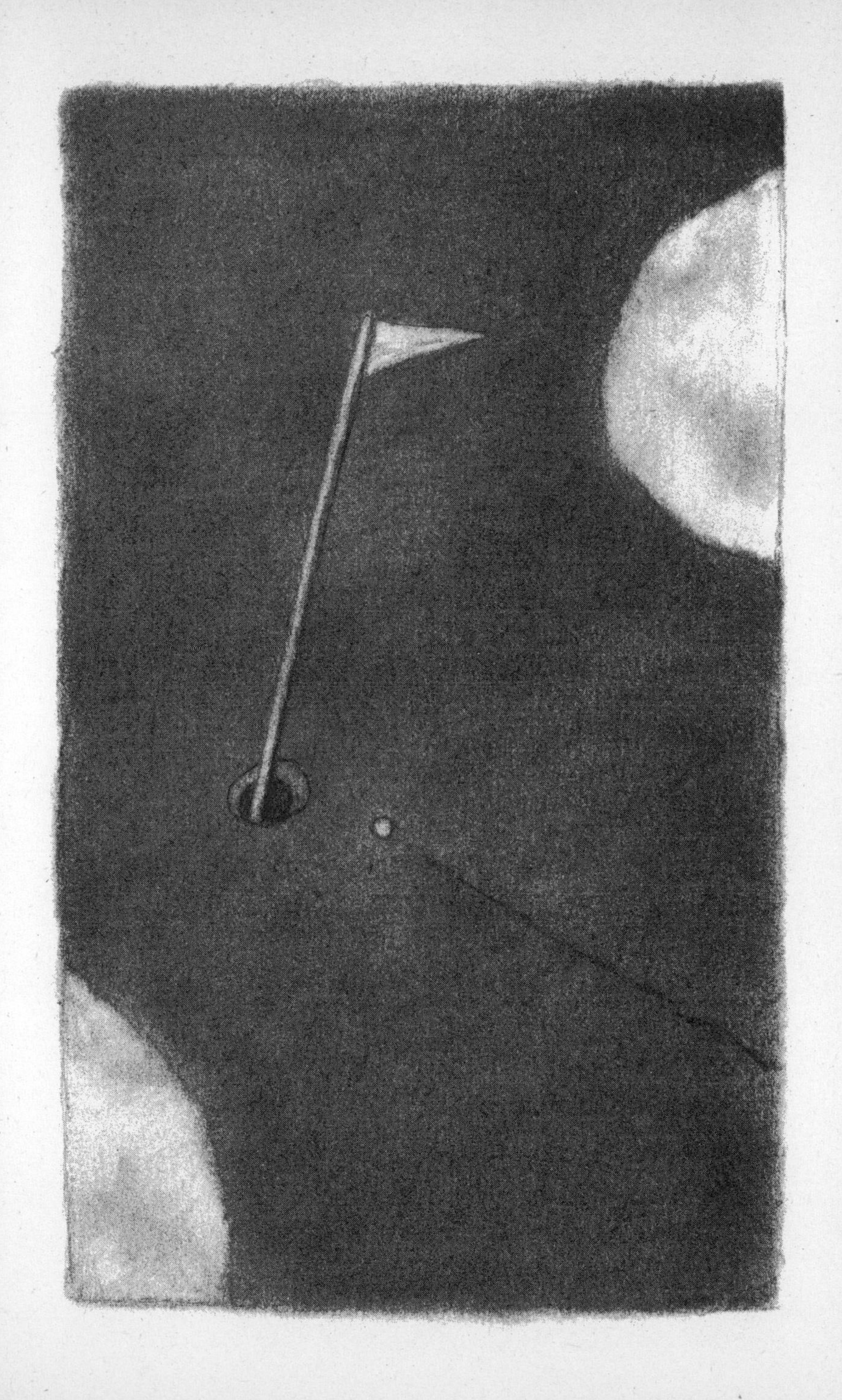

"No. You see, the idea is to start by having a very concrete intention or image of exactly what you want—to see and feel it. Then you let that intention become fainter and fainter within you so it remains just as a *feeling*. What you're left with is a very faint feeling on the level of your intuition, your heart. When you actually get up to swing, the only thing you have in your mind is your superfluid swing, but on the feeling level that intention of what you want to do is still there. It's most important you don't try to analyze that feeling—that you just trust in the cosmic computer and let it happen in its own natural and spontaneous way."

"I'm not sure I'm going to be very good at this kind of thing. I mean, feeling on the level of the heart. I like the vision stuff, but this feeling thing, I don't think it's for me."

"Try it, Mr. Smith. I want you to start with it when you putt. We'll go through a few procedures and then, if it works for you, stick to it."

"Yeah, okay. I'll give it a try."

"Let me ask you something. Have you ever had the feeling when you're putting that you know for certain the ball is going to go into the hole? Do you sort of see it in your mind before you actually make the putt?"

"Yeah," Smith said. "I've had that feeling a few times. It's great. Everything feels so simple, so right. I knew even before I stood up to the ball that I was going to make it."

"Describe to me what happened when you had that experience."

"How do you mean?"

"All the details. Did you survey the green beforehand? What did you feel just before you swung the putter?"

"I guess I did the normal things like check the break

and slope, but it was different because I kept thinking to myself, 'This is easy, a piece of cake.' "

"That experience is what I call the **Q formula.** It has two parts. The first part involves using a simple, fairly standard routine to gather all the relevant data. Let me show you."

Smith watched St. Clair carefully remove a putter from his bag and walk onto the practice green. He dropped a ball at his feet.

"Look at the other side of the green opposite your ball," Linc said as he walked about ten feet past the ball and crouched down facing Smith. "Survey the grade of hill, the slope, and any breaks in the green. With my own personal Q formula, I like to walk around the hole and really feel all the undulations of the ground. Some people take one look and putt. It's important to find out what works best for you." He stood and walked back to his pupil.

"Keep it natural," he said, "just a simple routine. Once you've gathered your key information, you come to the second part of the Q formula. You've already described it to me."

"I have?"

"Yes. The second part of the formula has to do with feeling. You must stop analyzing. You must feel in your heart that it's 'a piece of cake' and trust that you can make the putt. Why do you think that you don't have that experience all the time?" he asked.

Smith shrugged. "I don't know."

"That feeling of confidence," Linc explained, "only comes when your internal rhythm is linked to the cosmic computer, when you're able to have broad comprehension and focus simultaneously. The whole and the hole," he joked. "The important thing in putting is to stay simple and allow yourself to be on the deepest inner level."

Smith smiled vaguely. "One thing," he asked. "How does this relate to Q vision?"

"Q vision is a tool to help you create an effective Q formula. Before you swing you see the path of the golf ball, see the ball roll along that path, and feel the breaks it will take and the speed at which it will travel. I want you to imagine that *you are the ball.* Don't hurry this process; you need to see the putt as much as possible and, if you can, feel it." Linc laughed. "If you could taste and smell it, that would also be good."

Smith looked at his teacher in bewilderment. The guy was always throwing him curves. He repeated St. Clair's words, "Smell and taste the ball? Smell and *taste* it?"

"I even want you to *hear* the ball plunking into the hole. Don't think about taking your putt until you hear that sound—'plunk.' "

Smith had to laugh.

"The whole process shouldn't take very long. You can do it while the other players are lining up their putts."

"There's nothing I hate more in a game than people who take too long putting."

"I agree. Some players take an unnecessarily long time. They think that's the way to do it because that's what they see on TV. But," Linc warned, pulling the brim of his hat down to shade his eyes, "don't rush it, either. You should be relaxed and feel the path as many times as you like; don't strain, be simple. Just before you putt, let that vision become fainter and fainter so that it becomes just a feeling on the level of the heart, nothing more complicated than that. It's a kind of trust that everything is going to work out, knowing that the cosmic computer *will* do everything. When you actually come to putt, the only thing in your mind is your superfluid swing and some faint feeling of trust. All *you* have to do at this point is swing your club and hear the ball roll in the cup. You know that sweet sound of a ball dropping into a cup?"

"Sure—'plunk.' "

"Right," Linc said, grinning. "The ball is just going to move in a superfluid flow toward the hole and drop in."

"A superfluid flow into the hole," Smith said wonderingly. "I like that. I can see that . . . and feel it and hear it. Yes," he repeated under his breath, "I like that."

"Once you get the hang of it in your putting, then I want you to do the same thing in pitching and chipping. Feel the superfluid flow with all your senses, okay?"

"Okay, I can handle some of this sensory stuff, but I'm still not sure about seeing with my heart."

"Don't worry about that right now. It will come naturally."

"If you say so," Smith said doubtfully.

"Right now I want you to have fun with this exercise. You should always have the thrill of knowing that you can make a long putt, knowing you can chip into the hole from off the green. It should always be a joy for you."

"Putting and chipping a joy?" Smith made a face. "I always get nervous when it comes to my short game."

"Once you learn to trust in your feeling level, you'll have the same effortless, superfluid feeling in all your shots."

Smith grinned widely. "I'd like that."

"I have one more exercise for you today: When you're at the driving range, I want you to tee up three balls in a row." Linc held up three fingers.

"Not on top of each other like you did the other night?" Smith's voice shook.

St. Clair gave him a wry smile. "That won't be necessary. You will be hitting the balls one at a time."

"Oh, of course," Smith said as if he had realized it all along.

"Now, with the first ball"—he folded down two fingers so only one was erect—"I want you to hit it with a seven or eight iron with your normal superfluid swing. Before you come up to the ball use your Q vision—see, hear, and feel the superfluid flow of the ball moving toward your target. When you have a clear image of it, forget it, *then* approach the ball and go through your superfluid swing."

Linc held up two fingers. "On the second ball, I want you to do the same thing, only this time, tone down the power of your swing by about twenty-five percent and pick a target about seventy yards away—in other words, about half the distance you normally hit the ball. Now you want a little lighter, a little more delicate superfluid swing," he said. "What you'll find is that, with this lighter swing, the ball may even go farther."

Then he held up three fingers. "And finally, on the last ball, tone down the strength of your swing by another twenty-five percent, and aim for a target about a third of your normal distance away. In this way you'll improve your sensitivity to superfluid flow. Notice the feeling within you. Is it consistent with the shot as you imagined it beforehand? If not, repeat the exercise until the outer swing is the same as your inner feeling. It's a paradox: Even with a slower, lighter swing, the ball actually goes farther. This exercise will develop your trust in an effortless, superfluid swing. Did you get all that?"

"I did," Smith replied promptly.

"All great golfers know that it's very important to have a good feeling for the swing, to know where the club head is at all times and its precise angle. But it takes a very long time to acquire such a feeling by using classical methods. The intellect is so involved in analyzing one aspect that it forgets about others. With Q vision *you* care only about the feeling, and the cosmic computer takes care of the details. It's very easy and, as your trust in it grows, it will dramatically increase both your distance and accuracy."

Smith crowed, "You think I can hit the ball even farther?"

"Yes, but remember," Linc warned, "you made a commitment to me not to worry about distance."

Smith's face fell. "You're right, I did."

"It's very important," Linc counseled earnestly. "If distance comes automatically because your swing is more and more superfluid, that's fine, but *no effort* on your part, right?"

"Right," Smith agreed.

"And remember." Linc grinned. "Dance with the club."

"Dance with the club?" Smith clutched his club to his chest and walked off, humming a dance tune from his youth.

Practice Drills for Chapter 4

1. Practice **Q vision** in putting by first placing the ball a foot from the hole. Take a step behind your ball and see the path you want it to take. Don't hurry this process. Be sure to step backward and both see and *feel* it. *Hear* the ball plunking into the hole. Be simple—everything is on the level of feeling. Use all your senses to make your feeling as vivid as possible. Then move the ball a few feet back from the hole, and go through the entire routine again. Gradually work yourself into longer and longer putts. After each putt, pay close attention to whether or not the path, rhythm, and feeling of the putt replicated what you had imagined.

2. Use your **Q vision** to develop your own personal **Q formula** for putting. The first part involves finding a particular sequence, a standard routine to gather all the relevant data. The second part of this formula has to do with feeling: Just before you are about to make the putt, you must stop analyzing. Relive your "piece of cake" experience; simply trust that you can't miss the putt. This confidence comes when you're able to be on the deepest inner level.

3. Once you've established your **Q formula** for putting, use your **Q vision** to create a **Q formula** for all your shots. Step behind the ball, see the target—for instance, a small patch of ground on the fairway or a spot on the green where you want the ball to land. Establish a target area with 80 percent of your normal distance capacity, not more. This will ensure a *confident, effortless swing.* Imagine the flight path the ball must take, and finally see and feel yourself effortlessly swinging the club. When you have a clear mental image of the ideal shot, think about it no further. Let the thought remain as only a faint feeling. When you step up to the ball to swing, have only one concept in your mind: superfluid flow. Continue this exercise until you become familiar with your own simple, standard routine. It should be so automatic and natural when you're playing that you don't think about it. This is your personal **Q formula**.

4. At the driving range, tee up three balls in a row. Hit the first ball with a seven or eight iron, using your normal superfluid swing. Remember the moment of rest at the top of your backswing. Pick out a specific target, use your **Q vision**, see and feel the ball move toward it. Do the same thing with the second ball, only this time tone down the force of your swing by about 25 percent. Use a little lighter superfluid swing. Make it a little more delicate. Finally, on the last ball, tone down your swing by another 25 percent. This will improve your sensitivity. When you finish, go back to your normal superfluid swing.

5. Make up an **advanced Quantum scorecard**. As directed in the practice drills for Chapter 2, take a normal scorecard and use the vertical columns to note whether the swings were Q (Quantum) swings or C (classical) swings, only in this case use a scale of +3 to −3 to give a finer graduation to your feeling of whether the swing was quantum or classical. A purely **Quantum swing** in which you gain energy would be a +3 swing, and a poor classical swing in which you lose energy would be −3. At the end, add up all the numbers and then divide the total by the number of swings in order to get your **advanced Quantum score.**

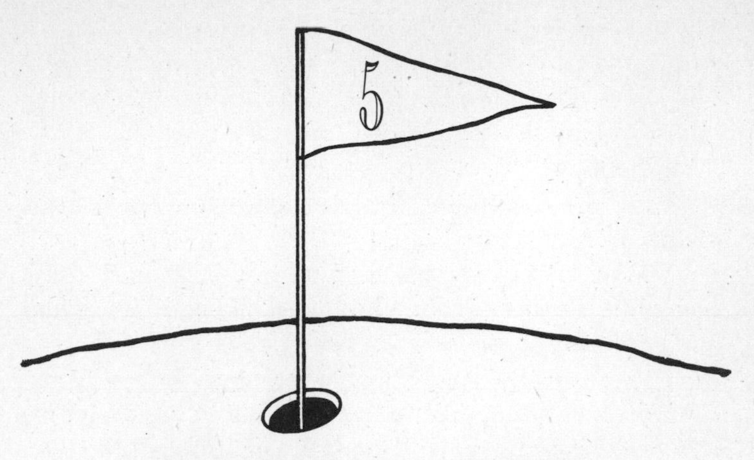

FINDING YOURSELF: THE COSMIC COMPUTER

Smith's bag was slung over his shoulder as he raced toward the practice area. His clubs rattled against each other in the bag.

"Mr. Smith, Mr. Smith." Before Smith could find St. Clair, the young assistant intercepted him. "Sir, Mr. St. Clair asked me to tell you he might be late today. He's got a mare giving birth at the farm, and he wants to be there."

"What?!"

"His mare, sir. She's foaling."

"I see," huffed Smith, but he didn't at all see why a pregnant mare should usurp his lesson time. As he slowly walked back to the clubhouse, Linc stepped out of a grove of trees.

"Ah, there you are, St. Clair," Smith grumbled. "I was waiting for you."

There was a congenial expression on the teacher's face.

He removed his straw hat and held it reverently in his hands. "Tell you what, Mr. Smith," he said. "I'll give you some extra time today to make up for your waiting and to celebrate."

"Celebrate?"

"Yep," Linc replied. "Best colt that's come out of this county in forty years."

"You're really into this farming . . . or should I say, animal thing, aren't you?" Smith asked, both fascinated and confused by his teacher's sideline.

"Oh, you could say I appreciate the perfection of nature in all its forms," Linc said, tucking a club under his arm. He leaned over and placed a ball on a tee, then turned and walked about twenty yards away.

Out of what appeared to be sheer high spirits, the teacher threw his hat high in the air and let forth with a wild yell that made the hair rise on Smith's arms. St. Clair swung the club several times around his head and ran full speed toward the ball. At the last moment he turned his shoulders sideways and took a perfect swing at the ball, looking like an Indian shooting a bow and arrow from a galloping horse. The ball traced into the blue sky, hooking sharply as it traveled some 350 yards in the air and then went another 50 to 75 yards on the ground, rolling past the edge of the practice range.

Smith breathed deeply, feeling the exhilaration of Linc's show.

"There's only time to go for the best," Linc said, his bright eyes shining. "If that's where you put your attention, it just naturally comes back manyfold." He laughed softly. "It's a question of the highest first."

"Yes," Smith said, nodding thoughtfully. "Well." He paused, somehow glad that he had good news to report today. "I wanted to tell you, I think I'm catching on. I'm really getting the feeling for this **Q vision** stuff. I hit in the seventies today. I almost got par." He shook his head. "It was plain fantastic!"

Linc's smile broadened. He retrieved his hat and plunked it on his head. "That's just how it should be," he said. "How was your **Q score**?"

"Around ninety percent, and that included my putting. Good, don't you think?" Smith was clearly pleased with himself.

St. Clair smiled. "Yes, very good."

"You promised to tell me about some new techniques today."

"I did," Linc said cheerfully, settling the straw hat on his head. The jewel-like feather fanned gently in the breeze as he looked up at the enormous shiplike clouds sailing in the blue above them. Smith, too, looked up, and they stood together in companionable silence.

"You'll learn several important points today," Linc said, looking at Smith. "They all come under the category of **finding yourself**. This is the fifth and final fundamental of Quantum Golf. If you remember, you already have: **frame of mind, flow, focus,** and **feeling**."

"I was hoping that by now I could learn something a little more sophisticated than a fundamental," Smith said. "I mean, fundamentals are for hitting the ball straight, and I'd like to learn some techniques for hitting an intentional hook or slice, or a knockdown or cut shot—you know, special shots that are used by more advanced golfers."

Linc laughed softly. "Mr. Smith," he said, "the most difficult shot there is is to hit the ball straight and true, but if you'd like me to show you some special shots . . ." He paused. "I think I can remember a few unusual shots I've had to make in tournaments. Did you have anything particular in mind?"

"Well, yes," Smith replied quickly. "To start with,

when I was playing on the tenth hole, my ball rolled up and stopped behind a big tree and I couldn't decide whether to try to hit over it or around it."

The pro nodded. "Let's take a cart out and we can deal with the shot on the spot." He called to his assistant, who was not far behind them, waiting beside a white golf cart. The boy brought the cart over to them and put their bags in the back. Linc and Smith drove around the back of the clubhouse and out onto the fairway of the tenth hole.

The fairway was bordered on both sides with a long stand of tall oaks scattered with some pine and graceful river birch. In the very middle of the fairway, guarding the right side of the green and about 125 yards from the hole stood an enormous, spreading oak like a gnarled old sentinel. Farther up, only 15 yards from the right edge of the green, stood another tree, a sculptured catalpa whose branches dripped with creamy blossoms. On the left side of the green was a long, deep, oval sand trap.

The men got out of the cart, and Smith walked over to a spot where both trees were between himself and the hole, about fifteen yards in front of the old oak.

"It was right here," he said, pointing at the grass beside his feet. "I just couldn't do anything. Even if I could get the ball over the top of that big tree, there is still the other one to get around."

"Drop a ball where yours lay earlier," Linc suggested.

Smith reached into his pocket and placed a new ball on the ground.

St. Clair seemed to be enjoying himself. He surveyed the lie for a minute or two and then went back to the cart and took out a club. As he walked back, he said, "There are several ways you can play this. The first is more classical, and the second is a little more quantum.

Since you're all fired up about shot-making, I'll show you the more complicated way first."

He then lined up his shot directly at the hole. "First," he said, "you must put the ball a little forward of your stance. This will ensure that the club strikes it on the upstroke and that it rises over the first tree. Next, you must make sure that your swing has an inside-out path. This will cause the ball to hook around that second tree and descend on a lower trajectory so it will pass under the branches . . . without knocking any of the flowers off," he added with a straight face. "To do this you have to put your right foot back and align your shoulders so they're pointing to the right of the target. The club face should still be aiming directly at the target. Next you move your hands slightly forward of the ball. You might think that this would counter putting the ball forward in your stance, since it does usually result in a lower trajectory, but in this case what is most important is to strike the ball well. I hope all this is perfectly clear?"

Smith scratched his head. Inside-out path . . . lower trajectory—he couldn't make any sense of it. Frustrated, he merely nodded at St. Clair.

"Good, now let's see if my calculations are accurate. If I'm off by even a quarter of an inch either way, it could result in disaster." Linc stepped up, checking each part of his stance and alignment, and then swung the club. The ball rose sharply and sailed high over the big oak. It descended in a gradual arc that hooked at the last part of its descent just under the flowering branches of the second tree and rolled onto the green, stopping about fifteen feet from the hole.

"You did it!" Smith exclaimed.

"It's not all that hard," Linc countered. "It only takes about twenty years of mechanical practice," he said, grinning at Smith's crestfallen expression. "Another method, for those who have mastered Quantum Golf, is to hit the ball perfectly straight."

"Straight?" Smith was incredulous.

"Yes, watch." Linc put another ball down in exactly the same spot as the first. He then began setting up to the ball, aiming far left of the hole toward the forest of trees.

What was he up to now, Smith wondered, quantum tunnelling?

St. Clair made a smooth Quantum swing. The ball went straight and true to the left, directly toward the middle of a large pine. With alarming accuracy it bounced off the trunk of the tree at an angle that propelled it over the sand trap. It landed on the green and rolled within three feet of the hole.

Linc looked up at Smith. "Like to give it a try?"

Smith frowned, his foot tapping the fairway as he adjusted his thinking. He sighed mightily. "I think you're right," he said. "It might be better for me to stick to the fundamentals a while longer. I'll master special shots later."

"Exactly, Mr. Smith. Once you own the fundamentals of Quantum Golf, these simple variations are not hard to learn, but you're now at the moment of **finding yourself.** Finding yourself is all important," he said. "It is what gives you deep-down confidence in your ability, confidence in your self, *Self*-confidence. If you can't even have the experience of your Self, then what on earth can you have confidence in?"

"Aah . . . I don't know. Nothing much, I guess."

"Exactly. If you act from a more superficial level of life, the results will be superficial. And if you act from a deeper level, the results will be more profound. The deeper you're able to go, the more profound the results.

"As I've said, classical golf directs all attention to the

surface levels of golf—parts such as the grip, the stance, et cetera. But remaining on the classical level gives ever-changing results, the ups and downs of golf. You're blowing in the wind with no roots to ground and nourish you. Every small alteration in your mood affects your game."

He looked at Smith, who nodded in silent agreement.

"The mind," Linc said, "has its attention only on the surface level, and then what you're failing to take into consideration as your priority is *the unchanging, reliable inner being* of the individual who is swinging the club."

As Smith listened, he again glanced up at the sky that wrapped all around them. It had an overwhelming appeal that contrasted vividly with New York's postage stamp skies, framed as those were by cement and steel.

"Classical golf," Linc continued, "is actually a part of Quantum Golf. Classical golf deals primarily with the swing and the outcome of the swing. Quantum Golf provides a complete understanding of all aspects of golf: the golfer, the golf swing, and the outcome of the swing. First and foremost it emphasizes the golfer, the inner man holding the club and taking the swing. It focuses on *his* inner rhythm, *his* inner being."

"So how do I go about all this?" Smith asked.

"Finding yourself has three parts, starting from the most concrete and working toward more abstract and powerful levels. The first part of finding yourself is finding your own game."

"Finding my game?"

"Yes, you have to learn to find your own game and play it. You must not, and I emphasize *must not*, worry about what anyone else is doing or how they are playing. Think only of what *you* want to do and how *you* want to play. Even if the person you're playing with consistently hits the ball ten or twenty yards ahead of you, you mustn't try to play the game he is playing. You must recognize *your own* game and stick to that. That doesn't mean you shouldn't go for it and take a daring shot at times, but the impetus should be based on your own game and not on trying to catch up or copy what someone else is doing."

"Shouldn't I try to keep up with my opponent?"

"Your real opponent is your own small self. When you worry about what another player is doing, you're engaging your small self in a dialogue of criticism, worry, and anxiety, all of which will hurt you. In order to keep your inner rhythm, you must **play your own game**. You know how far you can hit the ball, and you know what it takes to get to a specific target. Trying to adopt someone else's strategy is a tragic mistake in golf. It's always better in golf and," he added, "in life, to play your own game. Say it to yourself over and over—you can't say it enough: 'Play your own game.' 'Play your own game.' *'Play your own game.'* "

Smith's face was solemn as he took in Linc's words.

"Now let's look at the deeper aspect of today's lesson—**finding yourself**. Do you notice how different people take more or less time before their swing?"

"Sure."

"And you notice how some people get angry when they miss a shot, while others remain quite calm?"

"Uh . . . yeah." Was Linc referring to him? Well, admittedly, he got angry sometimes, but he'd played some guys who got so hot over bad shots that they made him look like Mr. Cool.

"It's very valuable to be able to recognize your own tendencies and how they relate to other people's tendencies," Linc said.

Smith regarded him attentively. This applied equally in business, he thought.

"We're all different and we can perceive certain different kinds of people, certain categories of body and behavior types."

"You mean like Type A and Type B behavior? I've heard about how hard driving and competitive Type A's are."

"Yes, Mr. Smith," Linc said wryly, "I'm sure you have, and a quantum method of body typing is something like that, only on a deeper, more profoundly individual level. It has to do with each individual's personal rhythm."

"Rhythm again, eh?"

"Yes, everyone has their own pace or frequency. For example, you've probably noticed that some people take a long time to make a decision. They tend to be slow and deliberate in their speech. They are very steady and stable in their manner."

"Sure, I know people like that. I usually have to hold myself back not to finish their thoughts for them."

"These people naturally have a slower frequency, a slower personal rhythm; they tend to be larger in size and heavier in build. On the other hand are individuals who possess the opposite tendencies. These people are ultra high-frequency types. They tend to be skinny and tall and —"

Smith interrupted enthusiastically, "They can't stop talking, ideas come a mile a minute, and they never sit still."

"Exactly."

Smith was interested. "What am I?"

"You would be in the upper to middle range of frequency. You are definitely *not* a slow-frequency type. The upper- to middle-frequency types have a medium-size, muscular body with good stamina and a strong constitution. People like this are frequently good speakers. You don't hesitate in making decisions and"—Linc gave a small smile—"you can easily lose your temper if you're not careful."

Smith frowned. Another reference to his temper. "Humph, I guess that isn't too hard to figure out."

Linc continued, "You probably have some trouble with your digestion, Mr. Smith, maybe a tendency towards ulcers."

Smith's brows rose in surprise. "I sure do!"

"All these tendencies affect your golf game."

"How?"

"In general, you want to hit the ball very hard—that's just the nature of your particular frequency. That's a tendency you need to control, and there are certain factors that can help you do it."

"Like what exactly?"

"Okay." Linc warmed to his explanation. "For example, your particular body type is very sensitive to heat, so it's important when you're playing golf to take measures to ensure that you don't get physically overheated. For you, too much heat could upset your game, while another person with a different body type might not be affected at all."

"Makes sense," Smith said. "But weren't you going to tell me today about a technique that will allow me to plug into my big Self, the cosmic computer?"

"Yes. It's the ultimate Quantum technique, and I want to share it with you, although it may appear a little unusual as a golf instruction."

Smith's eyes gleamed with anticipation. "I'm very interested."

"All right," Linc agreed. "I'll tell you." Still holding a club in his hand he began to make a rough drawing in a patch of the soft, dark soil that lay between the protruding roots of the big oak.

"Let's assume for a moment that our consciousness is

like the ocean. Thoughts arise within our consciousness like bubbles rising from the depths of the ocean." He began to draw a series of bubbles getting larger and larger.

"Normally we don't experience a thought until it reaches the surface of our mind. Our conscious mind is restricted to that level. But beneath the surface lies the deep, silent, wholeness of the ocean of consciousness. Imagine what it would be like if we could expand our conscious mind and experience thought at earlier stages of its development. This would bring us closer to the actual source of thought, which is an unbounded reservoir of energy and creative intelligence. This unbounded reservoir of potentiality is, in fact, the cosmic computer, our big Self."

"Sounds almost mystical," Smith said.

Linc laughed. "Think of it any way you like, but it works no matter what a person's beliefs are. It's very real, very powerful, and very easy to reach once you know how."

"Okay. How?"

"Through a simple process of inner self-development."

"But what do I *do*?"

"There are many different types of techniques for self-development," his teacher answered. "I meditate twice a day, and the meditation I practice fulfills all the criteria that apply to Quantum Golf."

"Look here, Mr. St. Clair," Smith bridled, "I have to tell you that I'm only interested if it will really help my golf."

"When we meditate," Linc replied, "we effortlessly go beyond, or transcend, our ordinary level of conscious thinking to quieter and deeper levels of consciousness, until finally we experience what we call the big Self, the cosmic computer, the cosmic rhythm. The ability to access your big Self is the whole point of Quantum Golf."

"I can't believe that's such a simple process."

"It's *very* simple," his teacher assured him, "but it's like any new experience: Unless you actually try it, you never really know what it is. You're no dreamer, Mr. Smith, you're a man of action. Give it a try. If you don't like it, you can drop it. But give it a chance."

Smith had learned other unusual things from St. Clair, and they'd all worked. He would try one more. "I guess that's reasonable," he declared. "If you're sure it'll help my game, I'll look into it."

"You came to me with one simple problem," Linc said, "your golf swing."

Smith nodded in agreement. "So?"

"So, in order to correct your golf swing, I first had to help you recognize the difference between a classical and a Quantum swing, right?"

"Right," Smith agreed.

"And in order to do that, you had to experience the **flow** of the Quantum swing."

"Superfluid flow, yes."

Linc nodded. "And to help you create an ideal swing, I had you **focus** on one aspect, the **Q point**."

"Correct."

"And finally you brought your experience to the level of **Q vision**, to the level of **feeling**—that most delicate, most powerful, subtle level of feeling that goes beyond the small self to the big Self, the cosmic computer."

"Yes."

"You see, Mr. Smith, in order to improve your swing, I had to get you to transcend, or go beyond, the level of the problem." Linc tipped his hat back on his head in a characteristic gesture.

"It's very difficult to solve a problem on its own level. You had to go to a more comprehensive and powerful level. As long as you were working on the classical level of the swing, you were stuck on that level. It was by transcending to a deeper level, toward the level of the source of thought, that you spontaneously began to develop a superfluid swing. Your muscles automatically began to work smoothly together; all the parts of your swing became integrated into a unified whole without your paying specific attention to them. Once you had the clear experience of that inner rhythm, that frictionless flow at the deepest level, then you began to trust in your cosmic computer, your big Self."

Smith pursed his lips juiciously. "That's true," he said.

"Your lessons are all just a journey to the big Self. Once you're able to have that experience, then everything becomes spontaneously perfect, your Q swing, your superfluid flow, your inner rhythm. **Finding yourself** is simply the natural conclusion to this journey."

"Okay," Smith said. "I'll look into meditation."

Linc extended his hand. "Fair enough."

Smith shook it. "But," he added, "*only* to improve my golf game, not my life."

Linc inclined his head to his pupil in a small bow.

"But, Mr. Smith," he said with a quiet smile, "golf is life."

Practice Drills for Chapter 5

1. When you play golf, make a tentative game plan for each hole: where you'd like to hit the first shot, the second, and so forth. Take into account how you feel, as well as the weather and your familiarity with the course. Make sure you're playing your own game. Is the first shot realistic for you? You may have to adjust your game plan after each shot, but always plan ahead according to your own skills on any particular day. Play your own game not somebody else's.

2. Look in the Reference section at the end of this book for more information on your particular body type.

3. Look in the Reference section for more information on meditation.

EPILOGUE

After breakfast at the golf club, John Smith placed his new straw Stetson on his head, jumped into the new car Mr. Smilek had lent him, and drove the purring vehicle over the dirt roads that led to St. Clair's farm. He marveled at the ride—his driving felt as effortless as his Quantum swing.

A cluster of tiny Sika deer watched from the side of the road as the gleaming car pulled up the winding lane. The dogs barked their welcome, and turkeys serenaded incongruously.

As he stepped from the car, the front door of the house opened and Linc appeared on the porch.

"Good to see you, Mr. Smith," he called, and walked down the small hill to meet him. Smith could hardly restrain his pleasure in the morning, in the drive, and in seeing his great teacher on this, his last day in Iowa.

"Please call me John," he said. They shook hands warmly.

Linc ushered him into the house. "Come in. Come in." The bright room had a fifteen-foot ceiling with exposed beams and pale walls made creamy by sunshine, except for one long wall that consisted of books from floor to ceiling.

"Quite a library," Smith remarked, carefully removing his hat.

"Oh, that's just the run-off." Linc chuckled and led him into a smaller room in which all four walls were booklined. There was an ancient stone fireplace in the middle of the north wall. Above the mantel hung a large and evidently very old, ornately framed portrait in oils that Smith recognized from reproductions in prints he'd seen in golf clubs all over the world. He stared at William St. Clair, captain of the Society of St. Andrew's Golfers, the Royal and Ancient Club, and of the Honourable Company of Edinburgh Golfers. The painting appeared to be an original.

He stared. Could Linc possibly be related to *this* St. Clair? The idea was fantastic, but not more surprising than anything else he'd learned on this trip.

Linc gestured to a well-padded rocking chair. "Please, sit down."

As Smith seated himself in the comfortable chair, he looked at his teacher, searching Linc's youthful face for a family resemblance. Surely not, he thought, and yet . . . ?

They spoke easily about the weather, farming, business, and Smith's family. He turned the new hat around on his lap, feeling strangely peaceful and happy.

"Do you feel up to a few practice holes?" Linc asked.

Smith's face registered pleased surprise. "With you?"

"Yes."

He rose quickly to his feet. "I'd love to."

"Good." Linc smiled. "We'll add some finishing touches to your game."

"Great," said Smith. "Shall we take your car or mine?"

"Oh, we'll just play here," Linc said.

"Here?"

"Yes." The Iowan reached over to a wooden hook on the wall and retrieved his own hat. Mashing it upon his head, he said, "I have three holes set up for myself. Just for fun."

Smith followed him out of doors and down the little hill toward a weathered cedar shed. The teacher opened the door, revealing bag after bag of clubs, some leaning in bunches against the walls. Smith recognized MacGregors from the 1950s, several valuable old putters in mint condition, including two Sportsman George Low Wizard 600's, a Bristol George Low Wizard 600, an early Ping Anser, and a variety of Wilsons. He eyed the clubs and estimated that they were worth a modest fortune. Linc took two sets of Pings from a cupboard and, shouldering the bags, they left the shed and walked around behind the house to a gently undulating, incredibly well-tended stretch of green.

Smith whistled and scratched his head. "Maybe this is heaven on earth after all!"

Linc grinned. "And no pesticides."

They walked to the first tee. After lining up his drive, St. Clair hit a perfect draw over 300 yards into the center of the fairway. His swing was obviously effortless. It appeared to be almost in perfect slow motion, yet the powerful crack as the club hit the little white sphere echoed in the still morning air.

"An incredible drive, Mr. St. Clair," Smith said. He adjusted his hat on his head. The thought that this man might actually be related to the venerable William St.

Clair haunted him. He remembered the pendulum and, using his three wood, hit the ball almost 230 yards straight down the fairway.

"Excellent," Linc said. "You've really improved your swing. You have your superfluid flow down pat."

Smith played down his performance as they walked along the fairway. "Oh, it was all right," he said, "but I hate to hit so darn short. Now I have to hit another three wood to get to the green," he complained. "You made such a long shot you only need an eight iron to get to the green."

"Remember," his teacher reminded him, "you're not to worry about distance."

As Smith meticulously began to line up his next shot, he stopped and stood up straight. With deliberate casualness he leaned his weight on the club, tipped his hat back on his forehead, and asked, "Tell me, are you any relation to William St. Clair of Roslin?"

Linc regarded him steadily for a moment. "You could say"—he paused—"we're almost one and the same."

Almost one and the same? What the dickens did he mean by that? Smith was baffled but put his attention determinedly on the pendulum; his breathing became regular, deep, evenly paced. His mind was clear for his shot.

Using **Q vision**, he then hit a perfect three wood that rolled to the edge of the green.

"Wonderful!" Linc exclaimed. "Isn't it more fulfilling to make the ball land just where you want it to go, instead of only trying to hit it as far as you can?"

"You're right," Smith said, relieved and quite happy to have reached the green.

Together they walked over to St. Clair's ball. Linc took out a short iron and hit a beautiful fluid swing. The ball made a perfect arc and landed a few feet from the

hole, where it bounced several times and then spun backwards within three inches of the cup.

Smith looked on with appreciation. "Amazing."

"Thank you, John. It's not me, though," Linc said, shrugging. "It's Quantum Golf."

They strode to the green and both men took out their putters. Linc went to the pin and marked his ball.

"Do you want me to hold the pin?" he asked.

"Yes, thanks." Smith walked past St. Clair and surveyed the slope and grade of the hill. It was about a twenty-five-foot putt. There was no break on the straight hill. Then he walked around the hole, making sure there were no unexpected bumps in the topography. After taking one last look from behind, he returned to his ball. Now he focused on the path of the ball and lined up his putter. The whole process was surprisingly quick.

Smith made his swing with a kind of lively intensity. His head never rose because he was too busy listening for the sound of the ball dropping in the hole. And it came.

He tossed his hat into the air. "A birdie!" he cried.

"Congratulations, John!" Linc called.

Even though his own ball was only about a foot and a half from the hole, Linc went through exactly the same setting-up procedure as Smith had done, and easily hit the ball.

"Did you notice," he asked, "that I went through my entire routine even though I had a short putt?"

Smith shrugged. "It did seem a little unnecessary."

"On the contrary," Linc said firmly, "it was absolutely necessary." He emphasized his words with a forefinger extended. "It's very important to go through every bit of your routine. It actually has to do with reinforcing neuromuscular pathways and connections. Every time you do it you set up a path for success. You don't want to go off this path. The more you walk on a path, the more defined it is and the easier the footing becomes. Gradually it becomes an effortless path on the level of feeling, one you don't have to think about, one you can rely on. It allows you to be totally confident when you hit the ball."

Smith's forehead furrowed in concentration.

"Did you notice that we both had the same score even though we played an entirely different game?" Linc asked.

"But yours was an easy birdie," Smith protested. "Mine was hard."

Linc laughed. "There is no 'easy' or 'hard' in Quantum Golf. The only thing that's important is playing your own game. If you leave your game and try and play mine, nothing will work for you."

"It is amazing," Smith conceded. "Even though you outdrove me by seventy yards, I got the same score!"

"That's because you played your own game and trusted in your **Q swing**. Shall we go on?"

"Yeah, this is great." Smith took in a deep breath of the richly scented, sweet air. He smiled in appreciation of the deep silence all around them, punctuated by the occasional lilt of birdsong.

At his next practice hole, a par five, Linc took out his driver and, as before, rocketed a perfect 300-yard shot into the center of the narrow fairway. Smith was slowly walking up to the tee with his three wood when Linc grasped his arm.

He held a club out to him. "Why not use this one?"

"But that's my driver. I thought I wasn't supposed to use that?"

"Today's an exception."

"You're sure?"

"Yes, go ahead. Hit a nice superfluid drive."

Smith was enthusiastic. "Right!" He hit the ball 260 yards with a slight fade and thought out loud, "Too bad it wasn't straight."

"Yes, but it was superfluid, wasn't it?"

"Yeah," he admitted, "it was smooth and easy."

"Then you can be completely satisfied."

"You're right," Smith said slowly, recognizing the truth. "It was definitely a Q swing. I guess in the last couple of days I've been spoiled by hitting such perfectly straight shots." He laughed and shook his head. "It's such a crazy game. A week ago I would have been happy just to hit well, and now it seems like I might actually reach par."

"You're improving," Linc said, "but you don't have to rush yourself. Progress comes naturally, one step at a time. Oh, you're securely on the road to hitting par or better on every hole now, but what is *really* important is that you keep your attention on your inner feeling of superfluidity. That's what will allow you to reach par."

Smith was eager for reassurance. "You think so?"

Linc replied, "I know so."

Smith took out his trusty three wood and hit an excellent fairway shot about 100 yards in front of the green. Unfortunately, the ball took a bad bounce and landed fifteen yards behind the silvery trunk of a tall elm tree on a downhill slope.

He was very frustrated. "What a rotten shot."

"It was a good shot," Linc contradicted him. "You had a perfect superfluid swing. We can't always control where the ball will land. Mother Nature gives and she takes. We will always be tested by both success and failure. It's all how we deal with it. Quantum mechanical is the name of the game."

They walked up to the teacher's ball. Linc took a two

iron from his bag and hit it squarely to the center of the green. The ball landed about twenty yards from the hole.

"Beautiful shot," Smith praised the professional.

"Thank you," Linc replied.

When Smith reached his ball, he pulled out a pitching wedge. "I hate downhill lies. I can never remember how I should hit them."

"The harder the lie, the more you must breathe easily and *relax* in order to settle into a superfluid swing. Classically speaking, you should adjust your stance to the particular lie, but this is secondary to keeping your attention on a superfluid swing. **Superfluid** is always the highest priority, especially in difficult situations."

Before he went up to the ball, Smith paused. He went through his superfluid swing in his mind. He then hit a perfect shot that landed almost beside Linc's ball.

"Excellent shot, John! I particularly like the pause at the top of your backswing."

At the green St. Clair putted first. He went meticulously through his entire procedure of putting and then gently stroked the ball down a long curved hill right into the cup.

"What a great putt," Smith said.

"Superfluid, eh?" Linc laughed. "Now it's your turn to do it. Okay?"

"Okay!" Smith took his time lining up the putt. His ball followed the same line as Linc's and rolled right into the hole.

"Fantastic! I love it!" There was wonder in Smith's voice. "Is it always this good?"

"Not always," Linc said as he leaned down and picked up a stray peacock feather from the grass. "Once in a while you'll revert back to the classical and lose it, particularly when you're at the first tee and want to make

a good impression on people watching you, but"—Linc twirled the long feather between his fingers and reassured his pupil—"not very often."

"I'd like to play an entire eighteen with you. I'm sure I could get par."

"You might at that," Linc said. "Good play is contagious. It really does help to play with another golfer who has a Quantum swing. What you see you become." He reached over to Smith and firmly placed the feather into Smith's hatband, where it waved like a banner. Then he picked an iron from his golf bag and walked to the tee. The hole was a par three with a wide, glassy pond immediately in front of the tee. The green was on the side of a hill about 180 yards away. Linc removed his hat and spun it to the side. He lined up the ball and smashed a high fade shot that stood out against the sky and then fell to the ground a few feet to the side of the hole.

Smith stood in silent appreciation. As he stood up after teeing his ball, drops of rain hit his face.

What's a little rain? he thought, and pulled the brim of his hat lower. He used his **Q vision** technique and saw the sixteenth hole in his mind. He made it into a great whirlpool. His job was simple, just put that tiny little white thing anywhere within a radius of twenty feet, and the big whirlpool would suck it in and down. He felt confident. He had a sense of time slowing down. An ocean of superfluidity flowed through him, through every cell of his body, through his hands and into the club, and from the club back into his hands again. The club hit the ball and made a sweet swishing sound, like a perfectly executed slalom turn in a spray of powder snow.

There was a rise in the green, so he couldn't tell exactly where his ball had landed. He didn't care. He felt great. He let his arms drop to his sides and leaned back and shut his eyes, opening his mouth wide and letting the rain fall into it.

Linc strode ahead of him to line up his own putt. As Smith walked toward the green, he began to worry that his shot had gone too far.

"A hole in one!" Linc called. "You got a hole in one!"

Smith couldn't believe it. He was stunned, disbelieving.

"This is great, John! Is it your first hole in one?"

"Yes," Smith replied.

"It sure won't be your last!" Linc exclaimed. "Now you're playing Quantum Golf."

SUGGESTIONS AND REFERENCES

For classical golf fundamentals:

Ben Hogan's book, the first I read on golf, taught me the classical fundamentals—grip, stance, etc. Even today it is the simplest and best introduction to classical golf. (To learn more about the fundamentals, I also recommend that you take advantage of the expertise of a qualified PGA or LPGA instructor.)

Five Lessons: The Modern Fundamentals of Golf by Ben Hogan, New York: Simon and Schuster, 1957.

For more information on body type:

Perfect Health is a wonderful, complete book on all aspects of quantum health and body typing. I also recommend *Quantum Healing* as an excellent book on health in general.

Perfect Health by Deepak Chopra, M.D., New York: Crown, 1990.
Quantum Healing by Deepak Chopra, M.D., New York: Bantam, 1989.

For more information on meditation:

More scientific research has been published on the Transcendental Meditation technique than on any other self-improvement program today and anyone can learn, regardless of age, educational background, or religious beliefs. I've practiced TM for a number of years and highly recommend it to all golfers.

Transcendental Meditation by Robert Roth, New York: Donald I. Fine, Inc., 1987.

I've spent many hours discussing the ideas and analogies used here with Dr. Keith Wallace, Chairman of the Physiological and Biological Science Department and Director of the doctoral program in Neuroscience at Maharishi International University in Fairfield, Iowa. He in turn gives credit to the founder of the university and of Transcendental Meditation, Maharishi Mahesh Yogi, for many of the original concepts. The following books provide excellent overviews of their ideas.

The Neurophysiology of Enlightenment by Robert Keith Wallace, Ph.D., Fairfield, Iowa: MIU Press, 1989.
The Body of Consciousness: The Body of Matter by Robert Keith Wallace, Ph.D., Fairfield, Iowa: MIU Press, 1990.